BROKEN WALLS

Caleb Rosado

Pacific Press Publishing Association
Boise, Idaho
Oshawa, Ontario, Canada

Broken Walls is part of the North American Division Series on church leadership. Additional titles in the series include:
Adventist Pastoral Ministry
A Guide to Marketing Adventism
Plant a Church, Reap a Harvest
Seeking His Lost Sheep

Edited by Marvin Moore
Designed by Bill Kirstein and Linda Griffith
Cover art by Lars Justinen
Typeset in 10/12 Century Schoolbook

The author assumes full responsibility for the accuracy of all facts and quotations cited in this book. Unless otherwise indicated, all Bible quotations are from the Revised Standard Version.

Library of Congress Catalog Number: 89-61515

ISBN 0-8163-0862-4

90 91 92 93 94 • 5 4 3 2 1

Contents

Dedication

Dedicated to Samuel Betances, my closest colleague and friend, who through the years has been "the wind beneath my wings."

Foreword

For the church it is the best of times and the worst of times—times of unprecedented danger, but also of unparalleled opportunity.

The Seventh-day Adventist Church, along with other evangelical denominations, is growing rapidly. A multitude of new believers from every nation, kindred, tongue, and people swells our ranks. We operate a network of universities, colleges, and schools. We direct a worldwide system of hospitals, clinics, and dispensaries. We own a publishing empire flung across the face of the planet.

In many respects, the church is rich and increased with goods. We can rightly point to evidences of the Lord's leading, as countries long resistant to our mission, due to entrenched political or religious systems, open up to the preaching of our messengers.

Yet alarms warning of grave peril to the church's identity and future sound amid the strobe lights of prosperity. Bigness is not an end in itself. What is the quality of our faith and witness? A revival of true godliness remains the greatest and most urgent of all our needs.

Many of the candidates for ministry come from among recent converts. Large numbers of our youth and young adults feel but a weak commitment to the church's mission, and frightening numbers retain ties to the church on no more than cultural grounds. We are winning a harvest of men and women—especially in developing nations—but we are failing to inspire and hold many of our brightest sons and daughters.

The church is in the world, and inevitably, the spirit of the age impacts upon us. Ours is an era of affluence coupled with gross selfishness. Material values drive the marketplace as well as more and more followers of the lowly Jesus. God's people need to hear again the Nazarene's call to discipleship— to a way of life in the world that renounces greed and extravagance.

We need to hear His claim to Lordship. In the midst of this secular age that glorifies men—and in the church, would glorify men in the name of Christ—we need to bow at the feet of the One who is the church's Head.

Many Christians no longer take membership in the church seriously. They neither sense its sacred privileges nor accept its responsibilities. Increasingly, they look on the church as a club that one can join, drop out of for a time, and rejoin at any whim.

In centuries past the church preyed upon people's fears and superstitions, holding members in religious chains by her supposedly divine prerogatives. Today our problem is just the reverse: Christians place altogether too low a value on the church.

And as always, the church confronts culture. Aspects of culture may be compatible with the gospel of Jesus Christ or neutral in relation to it. Frequently, however, the way of Jesus confronts and contradicts the patterns of culture.

Over the course of the centuries, the church fared poorly in this confrontation. Frequently she capitulated to culture, selling her birthright for a mess of pottage.

Nor has the Seventh-day Adventist Church challenged culture as she might. We have a heritage that instructs us and calls us to holy confrontation. Ellen White encouraged believers to disobey the fugitive slave laws. Other pioneers of the church supported the "underground railroad" for escaping slaves, and the young church gave its women a public role in preaching and leadership.

But in the twentieth century, we have not been as true as we should to this history and to the gospel on which it rests. Baseball was integrated before our churches. Many women and minority groups in North America—especially Hispanics—feel left outside the decision and leadership processes of the church. We frequently succumb to pressures from racism and tribalism instead of than refusing to give them a place in the communion of Christ.

We all grow up creatures of pride and prejudice, and our most deeply rooted pride is race. Where else will humanity find healing for the bitterness that divides it—White against Black and Black against White, men against women and women against men, young against old and old against young, rich against poor and poor against rich, learned against uneducated and uneducated against learned—unless they find it in the church?

With the rapid growth of the church, especially in Africa and South and Central America, the Lord is placing within our hands an unparalleled opportunity for a demonstration of the transforming power of the gospel. He seeks nothing less than the formation of His image in our midst—individually and corporately. What will we do with this opportunity?

Ephesians is *the* book of the church. Here we find what it means that the church is Christ's body. We see Jesus as Lord of the church. We learn the high privileges of membership and the responsibilities that accompany membership.

Ephesians tells us that the church impacts more than vertical relationships. While the individual reconciliation with God that the Cross has brought gives us entry into the church, once inside, we no longer stand alone. To our individual identity Christ adds a corporate identity. We become members *of one another* as we become members of His body. Horizontal relationships—our attitudes, words, and responses to other members of the body—demonstrate the degree to which we have submitted to Christ as Head of the body.

Dr. Caleb Rosado's study of Ephesians is timely, alert as the author is to the cultural pluralism in the Seventh-day Adventist Church today. The church urgently needs an ecclesiology—one that deals not only in classical formulations, but that brings theology into the most difficult area of all: human relations, the arena where culture rubs and merges and clashes with culture, the arena of color and smells and food and songs, the arena of our most deeply-rooted pride and prejudice.

Broken Walls marks an important milestone toward such an ecclesiology for the Seventh-day Adventist Church in these times.

William G. Johnsson, Ph.D.
Editor, *Adventist Review*
April 24, 1989

Preface

Ideas are products of their time. Insights into both the spiritual and social world come into being as a result of the changes in society. George Herbert Mead in his insightful little volume, *Philosophy of the Present*, tells us that we tend to interpret the past in terms of the needs of the present. Thus our unique present situation enables us to see things in retrospect that previous generations may not have seen.

This book and the insights that it brings into the study of Paul's letter to the Ephesians reflect the changes taking place both in the world and in the church. We no longer live in the agrarian society out of which the Adventist Church arose, but in a multicultural society with an international worldview. The needs of ministry in a culturally pluralistic society raise new questions about the mission of the church.

This book arose out of the pastoral needs of the All Nations Church in Berrien Springs, Michigan. Founded in 1979, it was the first church in the denomination to be deliberately established along multicultural lines to minister cross-culturally to representatives from some sixty ethnic groups. This posed a challenge. The prevailing models of ministry were based on the "homogeneous unit" principle of the McGavran School of Church Growth at Fuller Theological Seminary in Pasadena, California. This principle states that men like to become Christians without crossing racial, linguistic, or class barriers. As the founding pastor of the church, I felt that such a homogeneous and exclusive model of ministry would not do with a heterogeneous congregation in a culturally pluralistic society. I therefore developed an inclusive model of ministry based on the "heterogeneous unit" principle of church growth—the view that the *gospel challenges and empowers people to accept Christ across all social barriers.*

An inclusive theology that embraced the social and spiritual unity of Christians needed to be developed. Paul's letter to the Ephesians, the central theme of which is unity in diversity in Christ, provided the conceptual scheme. The letter makes clear that the problem of present-day Christianity is the same as the early church: uniting culturally diverse people (Jew and Gentile) in the same worshiping community. The content of this book began as a series of sermons to bring unity within diversity in the All Nations Church.

The fact that a Hispanic was both the first pastor of the church and author of this material is most significant. Hispanics, by their very biological and socio-historical development, are a multicultural people—the physical embodiment of European, African, and American Indian matrices.[1] Thus Hispanics are ideally suited to be ethnic bridge builders in a multicultural world. Out of this biological and sociocultural development, influenced by graduate work in sociology, I served as the catalyst for bringing to the church a new awareness of its need for a racially and culturally inclusive model of ministry. Thus this book represents a voice from the "silent minority" that for too long has been denied a voice in church polity and theological matters. It represents a new wind blowing through the stuffy, stale corridors of the church; the new wine of multiculturalism challenging the old wineskin structures of the church, in light of the social ferment taking place in society.

This book would not have been possible without certain influences in my life. I will mention first the courageous vision of Dr. Charles D. Joseph, then president of the Lake Region Conference, who had the foresight to establish a multicultural church in Berrien Springs, and called me back into the ministry to get it off the ground. Then there were the members of the All Nations Church, especially the original charter band of believers from some sixty-five countries, who early grasped the vision for an alternate model of ministry in Christianity and in Adventism, and gave me the freedom not only to experiment with their spiritual development, but to preach and practice the gospel biblically. The greatest influence in the development of the ideas for this book came from my long-time best friend, colleague, and former college roommate, Samuel Betances, professor of sociology at Northeastern Illinois University in Chicago, to whom this book is dedicated. Early in my ministry, Samuel forced me to take into account the influence of society on the church, and enabled me to come to grips with the power of a positive ethnic self-identity as a Puerto Rican and a Latino. It was he who first gave me an understanding of racism and cultural pluralism, both in society and in the church, and through his influence, I, too, became a sociologist. Last, I want to give special thanks to William G. Johnsson for kindly accepting my invitation to write the thought-provoking foreword to this book.

The subject matter of this book is approached from a sociological perspective. Neither individuals nor institutions exist in a social vacuum, isolated from the forces of the larger society. Nor is society a static entity, but an ever-changing one, the changes of which also impact the church. To understand the mission of the church, we must also understand its society, its human context, for it is here that the church carries out its mission. We can best understand the problems plaguing the church by understanding society, and how society helps or hinders the church's task of fleshing out the kingdom of God on earth. Sociology, the study of human social interaction, enables us to understand how to relate theology to human need.

It is my hope that the contents of this book may enable the church to break down the walls of racial hostility that Christ broke down 2,000 years ago, but which have been erected once again in our midst. Such a militant act will enable the church complacent to become the church triumphant.

---

1. See Caleb Rosado, "Bridging Ethnic Differences: Insights on Hispanics," *Message* 52:2 (May-June, 1986).

CHAPTER
One

Introduction[1]

The Christian church today faces the ever-increasing challenge of an interdependent, multicultural society. An agrarian society with a homogeneous orientation largely dominated human history until the mid-nineteenth century, when the economic base shifted from agriculture to industry, first in Europe, then in the United States, as a result of the Industrial Revolution. With industrialization, hordes of people, brought together from different walks of life and different ethnic origins, were forced to interact with each other and form some collective sense of existence. The industrial society, with the assembly line as a model of operation and uniformity as the goal, held sway until the late 1950s, when the information society had its beginnings. The information society ushered in the computer and the era of global satellite communications, which gave rise to an international perspective and a concern with diversity.

This shift in society from uniformity to diversity, with its broadening perspective from nationalism to internationalism, has impacted the church. The multicultural framework of our large urban centers is forcing the church to reevaluate its mission and become more inclusive. However, such change is not always a welcome friend, especially to conservative institutions such as churches and schools. In a time of great change, people tend to retrench and hang on to those exclusive values and traditions that give them a sense of security in periods of social upheaval. This is why many schools support the English-only movement in education, and why conservative Protestant churches espouse the "homogeneous unit" principle of church growth in which people can join the church without having to cross racial, social, and class barriers. These ideas are popular because the church, like its counterpart, the school, seeks to hang on to narrow social values and exclusive cultural traditions that fly in the face of human needs and have little to do with the claims of the gospel.

The new wine of multiculturalism

One of the basic premises of sociology is that no institution can be understood in isolation from the larger society of which it is a part. Institutions do not exist in a social vacuum, but are social-historical entities that influence, and are influenced by, their cultural milieu. As our society has changed from an industrial society concerned with nationalism and uniformity to an information society concerned with internationalism and cultural diversity, its ethnic makeup has also changed. Along with these changes has also come a declining white population and a corresponding increase in the minority population. This ferment of change, brought about by the "new wine" of multiculturalism, is putting pressure on the old "wineskin" structures of the church and society. And unless these brittle old ecclesiastical and societal structures are willing to make the necessary changes, the result will be social chaos—riots, disturbances, protests, boycotts, strikes, etc. Look around at the world today, and everywhere you will see the new wine of multiculturalism, the ferment of change, and the resulting sociopolitical turmoil—in the Soviet Union, South Africa, the Middle East, Sri Lanka, India, China, Yugoslavia, Armenia, northern Ireland, Spain, France, Latin America, Canada, New York, Boston, Miami, Los Angeles, Chicago, and the university campuses throughout this nation. *The number one problem confronting world society today is racial and cultural in-*

sensitivity—the new wine of racial/ethnic ferment in conflict with the old wineskins of White social structures.

Long ago Jesus gave us a most important principle that we have yet to put into practice—the principle of new wine in new wineskins. " 'No one puts new wine into old wineskins; if he does, the new wine will burst the skins and it will be spilled, and the skins will be destroyed. But new wine must be put into fresh wineskins' " (Luke 5:37, 38). A new age demands new methods and new structures, for the ferment of change cannot be contained in the old structures, but will burst them. It is the old problem of "new wine in old wineskins." This truism of Jesus is so clear that one wonders how people throughout the ages can continue making the same mistakes in the face of pervasive change. Yet Jesus Himself gave us the reason why people continue making the same perennial mistakes. In the very next breath He declared, " 'No one after drinking old wine desires new; for he says, "The old is [better]" ' " (verse 39). Jesus means that even when change is necessary, no one really wants to change; people still prefer the old. Some people would rather see social unrest, protests, disturbances, riots, and boycotts than change their self-preserved, sacrosanct social structures. When change is unavoidable, those in power desire change that won't alter the old structures. The result is a lot of fine rhetoric, but a lack of reciprocal action—the refusal by the majority to learn from the minority, in the same way the latter learned from the former. Such a reciprocal process will result in lessons of sensitivity and inclusiveness of others that will enable all to be of service to each other.

During this period of great social ferment, the "new wine" of multiculturalism in society is challenging the old "wineskin" structures of the church to live out the inclusive principles of the gospel in a way that is faithful to the claims of the gospel. The new redemptive order of the gospel demands an inclusive model of ministry based on the "heterogeneous unit" principle of church growth—*that the gospel challenges and empowers people to accept Christ across all social barriers.* Thus all of God's children are one and have equal access to God, for "there is neither Jew nor Greek [no division based on racial and ethnic differences], there is neither slave nor free [no division based on social class], there is neither male nor female [no division based on sex and gender]; for you are all one in Christ Jesus" (Galatians 3:28).

In view of the heterogeneous character of the church and of society, the church can no longer continue to utilize homogeneous models of ministry to carry out its mission. Both the needs of a multicultural society and the claims of the gospel demand a change in strategy. The implication of all this to the church is that as our society has changed, so also has the ethnic makeup of our churches. Along with these changes has also come an increasing demand for expressions of worship and musical forms that are multiculturally sensitive and inclusive.

Many find it difficult to be open to such inclusiveness, however, because as Christians we have been socialized in a faith that is highly normative as to what is appropriate behavior for the Christian. When the Christian faith, which is above culture, is connected with culture, the result is that certain cultural expressions are brought into Christianity and made an integral part of the faith.

Compassion

One word describes what is being discussed here: *compassion*—the ability to suffer with another with loving, caring concern. Compassion is the most basic principle in effective intercultural relationships and multicultural ministry, for it requires that, as a prelude to action, we take the role of another, that we view life from his/her perspective, and be sensitive to his/her experience. Failure to understand the experience out of which another group develops results not only in cross-cultural misunderstanding, but in "talking past one another." This is a major problem in intercultural relations. Karl Mannheim discusses the problem that two socially different groups often have in communicating.

Although they are more or less aware that the person with whom they are discussing the matter represents another group,

16

and that it is likely that his mental structure as a whole is often quite different when a concrete thing is being discussed, they speak as if their differences were confined to the specific question at issue around which their present disagreement crystallized. They overlook the fact that their antagonist differs from them in his whole outlook, and not merely in his opinion about the point under discussion.[2]

Let me illustrate this point. Some time back I was at a ministerial gathering at Oakwood College, where I was to give several lectures on multicultural ministry. Except for a dozen Hispanic pastors, the main body of some 600 pastors present were African Americans. One of the presenters was a former professor of mine, whom I had not seen since college days. He was white, and as we chatted about old times, he admitted to me that this was the first time he had ever attended an all-Black ministerial conference. The preliminary song service was under way when all of a sudden, in the midst of our conversation, he became aware of the enthusiastic singing and asked me, "Is this how they sing all the time?"

I said, in "perfect" English, "You ain't seen anything yet!"

"You know, Caleb," he replied, "we don't sing like this in *our* meetings."

I immediately realized where he was coming from. The enthusiastic, pentecostal-type singing of African-Americans is not always appreciated or accepted as an appropriate expression of worship by many Whites in the church. My former professor was reacting to the situation from his own perspective and cultural awareness.

Having had little exposure to the African-American worship experience, he overlooked the fact that the audience before him differed from his culture in their *entire experience*, and not merely in the expressive manner of their singing.

I decided to reverse roles and share with him a lesson from the pages of African-American history. "You have to realize," I said, "that when a people has been dehumanized by 200 years of slavery, their voice silenced, and their self-worth belittled; and when you add to that more than 100 years of discrimina-

17

tion, rejection, and loss of personhood in the urban centers of America; when such people find freedom in Christ, they are going to SHOUT, and let the whole world know what it's all about. What you see here," I continued, "is 300 years of pent-up human dignity and self-expression bursting forth in song!" I then added, "Dr. Martin Luther King, Jr., once said that 'three hundred years of humiliation, abuse, and deprivation cannot be expected to find voice in a whisper.' "[3]

He turned to me and said: "I understand now. I understand."

Effective intergroup relations and multicultural communication begin when we take the role of the other and seek to understand where that person or group is coming from, and not just the issue under discussion.

In view of the great diversity among groups on the one hand, and the close adherence of each to its own values and traditions on the other, one would think it best for each group to go its separate way and worship God according to its own tradition. That would be fine if the various ethnic groups were isolated and independent of each other. But today we live in a multicultural, interdependent world that influences all aspects of life.

Long ago Ellen G. White declared:

> There is no person, no nation, that is perfect in every habit and thought. One must learn of another. Therefore God wants the different nationalities to mingle together, to be one in judgment, one in purpose. Then the union that there is in Christ will be exemplified.[4]

Herein lies a most basic principle of cultural sensitivity, the principle of reciprocal learning—that no one group holds a corner on knowledge, but that we must all learn from each other in order to broaden each one's understanding of the universe. The fact that the values and traditions of one group differ from those of another does not make either inferior to or of lesser importance than that of the other. They are simply different, each one being relative to the cultural ambience out of which it arose. Each of these values and traditions should be respected and acknowledged as valid, as valuable for learning.

If we don't learn these lessons of multicultural sensitivity and inclusiveness here as manifested in our choices of leadership, worship, music, and fellowship, we may feel uncomfortable standing in the presence of that large multiracial body gathered around the throne:

> I looked, and behold, a great multitude which no man could number, from every nation, from all tribes and peoples and tongues, standing before the throne and before the Lamb, clothed in white robes, with palm branches in their hands, and crying out with a loud voice, "Salvation belongs to our God who sits upon the throne, and to the Lamb!" (Revelation 7:9, 10).

Such a shift in worldviews also challenges us, in our relations with people of other cultures and ethnic groups, to be more sensitive to their spiritual needs in a world that is in a constant state of flux. A new age demands a new type of Christian action—the action of compassion!

Ephesians, the letter for today

If one portion of Scripture especially speaks to the sociohistorical reality of the church today, it is Paul's letter to the Ephesians. Ephesians is truly a letter to "all nations." From beginning to end, it is pregnant with meaning, significance, and importance to the church, for its unifying theme is "unity in diversity in Christ." The late C. H. Dodd, the renowned British New Testament scholar, called Ephesians "the crown of Paulinism"[5]—the crown jewel in Paul's theology.

Ephesians was written to encourage Gentile believers in the new universalism of the gospel, which means that as a result of the saving action of Christ, all people—both Jew and Gentile—stand as one family before God.

Chapters 1 to 3 announce God's plan, hidden from the beginning of the world, to create a new humanity in Christ—a new community—that unites both Jew and Gentile and erases the impenetrable social and religious barriers that have previously divided humankind. This unity is to be made manifest through the church in an external, visible, caring community.

It is Paul's privilege, as well as ours, to be a chosen herald of God, appointed to reveal to humankind the mystery of God's love, which mystery is the revelation of God's plan that Jew and Gentile be united in Christ. This unity is to be seen in the church (chapter 3:7-13), the visible manifestation of God's new humanity.

Paul then prays that his audience may understand, appreciate, and experience God's great love for humanity that has made possible such unity of people in the church (chapter 3:14-21). Paul realizes that, because of the pressure of society, such a plan is most difficult for people to accept in practice, especially in light of what he will say in chapters 4 to 6.

These chapters are exhortative, bringing forth conclusions that follow for the Christian life. Entrance into this new humanity is through baptism—a dying to the old and a rising to the new. This unity does not mean sameness and uniformity, however. Therefore God has given to the church a diversity of gifts, in harmony with the diversity prevalent in the church, that will not only edify the church but bring it to the fullness of maturity in Christ (chapter 4:1-16). (The gifts in Ephesians are different from the gifts in Corinthians and Romans. Here the focus is on the church universal and the gifts that make for unity in diversity in the church—the new humanity of God. The spiritual gifts in the other passages focus on the individual Christian and the gifts he receives.)

This new maturity in Christ results in a true renewal of life, motivated by a loving concern for fellow members in the church (chapter 4:17—5:20). This new spirit of oneness is especially to be made manifest in the home, where often the greatest disunity in Christ takes place, through the practice of domestic virtues, reflective of Christ's action on behalf of His church (chapter 5:21—6:9). This spirit of unity will also show itself in a courageous combat with the powers of darkness (chapter 6:10-17). We are not to evade the struggle, but meet it head on, not in our own strength and armor, but in the strength and armor of the Captain of the Lord's host.

The letter ends with a request for prayers and a final blessing, because such unity as Christ desires to bring to the church cannot be made manifest without much prayer and God's blessing.

This is the message of Ephesians, unity in diversity in Christ, a message that must be made visible in the church.

<hr />

1. Part of this introduction was published as an article, "Multiculturalism: A Challenge for the Church," in *Journal of Music Ministry* 16:1 (January-March, 1989), pp. 3-5.

2. Karl Mannheim, *Ideology and Utopia* (New York: Harcourt, Brace World, Inc., 1936), pp. 279, 280.

3. Martin Luther King, Jr., *Why We Can't Wait* (New York: The New American Library, Inc., 1963), p. 16

4. Ellen G. White, *SDA Bible Commentary* (Washington, D.C.: Review and Herald, 1954), vol. 2, p. 1029.

5. Quoted by Henry Chadwick in "Ephesians," *Peake's Commentary on the Bible*, edited by Matthew Black and H. H. Rowley (London: Thomas Nelson and Sons, Ltd., 1962), p. 980.

CHAPTER

Two

The Problem of Unity in Diversity

The letter to the Ephesians, the letters to the Colossians and the Philippians, and the letter to Philemon are generally known as the "captivity epistles" because they were written while Paul was in prison. Christian tradition says that Ephesians was written during Paul's first imprisonment in Rome. He was released for about two years and arrested again. He then wrote the pastoral epistles (1 and 2 Timothy and Titus) and was probably beheaded around A.D. 67.

A focus from prison

I have never had the privilege of being in prison. I say "privilege," because not all who have been sent to prison deserve to be in prison. What we need to understand is the "prison principle." Let me illustrate this principle by means of a bell-shaped curve.[1]

Most people in society are moderately good, in the sense that they conform to the way life is organized in any given society. Some conform better than others, or live such lives as to serve society in a positive way. These are the "good." Others

THE PRISON PRINCIPLE BELL CURVE CHART

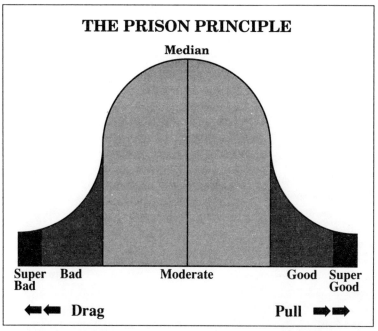

have some difficulty conforming and tend to engage in negative behavior. These are the "bad." Most societies can tolerate a large number of people who are good and others who are bad. There are two types of people, however, that society cannot tolerate: the "super-bad" and the "super-good." The first act as a "drag" on the system, the second as a "pull." Both are disruptive elements, for they move the system at either end of the social behavior continuum in a direction it does not want to go. Thus, they both violate the first commandment of social life: the system must be preserved at all costs.[2] The result is the prison principle: *Every society tends to incarcerate those who disrupt the system.* Thus, the same society that convicts a Charles Manson or a Barabbas will also convict a Martin Luther King, Jr., and a Jesus Christ. Society sets up the system of incarceration to restrain not only the super-bad, but

23

also the super-good—all those at either end of the spectrum who alter the status quo or seek to bring about change in a rapid or dramatic way, such as the student protesters in China during the spring of 1989. While the majority of prisoners tend to come from the bad end of the continuum, prisons have seen their share of persons from the good end—people like John Huss, Jerome, Martin Luther, Joan of Arc, Gandhi, Martin Luther King, Jr., Cesar Chavez, Dorothy Day, Nelson Mandela, Desmond Tuto, the twelve apostles, the apostle Paul—even the Son of God Himself, Jesus Christ of Nazareth. All of these were served with prison sentences, and some even bore the title of "ex-con."

This principle has tremendous implications for the role of the church in society. In Old Testament times prophets were stoned because their message contradicted the values and status quo of society. Society had the choice of obeying the message or getting rid of the messenger. With but few exceptions, it opted for the latter. This is why Jesus was killed. His message was most disruptive to society. Caiaphas clearly recognized this when he declared, "Better for one man to die than for the entire nation to perish" (John 11:50, my free translation). John then states, "From that day on the Jewish authorities made plans to kill Jesus" (verse 53, TEV).

The state will only take action against the church when the teachings and practice of the church go contrary to the values and behavior of society. As long as the church serves as the gatekeeper of the values of society, blessing the actions of the state, as has been the historic stance of Protestantism in the United States, the Christian church will never undergo the kind of persecution at the end of time described in the book of Revelation, for it has accommodated its faith to safeguard the status quo. But let the church raise its voice in a prophetic posture, challenging social injustic and the violation of the principles of God's kingdom on earth, and it will incur the wrath of the dragon. "The dragon was angry with the woman, and went off to make war on the rest of her offspring, on those who keep the commandments of God and bear testimony to Jesus" (Revelation 12:17). This is more than just keeping the

Ten Commandments and having the prophetic gift, as Seventh-day Adventists tend to believe. It means to stand with Jesus and prophets like Elijah, Jeremiah, and John the Baptist against the prevailing relgio-political system, and challenge the very structures of society as incompatible with the kingdom of God! The role of a prophetic movement is a dual one of annunciation and denunciation—not only to announce the future, but also to denounce the present. As long as it only announces the future, no church or movement will incur the wrath of others. But let it also denounce injustices in the present, and martyrdom will be around the corner. Such was the posture of Paul, and the very reason why he was now in prison.

Prison tends to give one plenty of time—time for meditation and reflection on such questions as, "What am I doing here?" "What have I done to deserve this?" "What are the implications of my imprisonment to myself, my family, and to others?" Such were the questions that Paul must have mulled over in his mind, especially when he remembered that he himself had been a bounty hunter, searching out Christians and throwing them into prison (see Acts 8:3). Now here he was, the biggest persecutor of the church, himself in prison, as a result of persecution by others. This wasn't the first time he had been in prison. "Paul spent time in prison in almost every community he founded."[3] In 2 Corinthians, for example, he declared that he had suffered "far more imprisonments" than his accusers (11:23).

Paul now had time to reflect on the many events that led to his present circumstances: his early enthusiasm to destroy the fledgling church; his conversion experience on the way to Damascus; his three years in the wilderness learning more about the One whose followers he had been persecuting, redirecting his values, and setting his priorities straight; his experience with the church in Jerusalem and how at first they did not want to accept their former persecutor as their representative to the nations; his call to be an apostle to the Gentiles; his three missionary journeys during which countless churches were established among the Gentiles, as the gospel

25

spread throughout the known world; the many letters he had written to these young churches, encouraging them in the Lord and giving them the essentials of the Christian message—all matters of serious reflection.

The problem of unity in diversity in Christ

In all this reflecting, Paul realized that the biggest problem lay in the inability of Jewish Christians to accept Gentile Christians as equal partners in Christ without accepting the whole religious, cultural baggage of Judaism. Jewish Christians conceded that the Gentiles had indeed responded to Christ, but they still treated these Gentiles with a better-than-thou attitude. Paul saw this lack of unity in Christ as the biggest obstacle before the church. Thus the biggest threat to the church's survival beyond the first generation came from within, not from without. He therefore did everything he could to bring about the necessary change.

By means of his letters Paul sought to bring about a proper understanding of the new humanity God intended to see reflected in the church. In Romans he spoke of the Gentile being grafted into the vine of God so that both Jew and Gentile could become one new vine in Christ. In Corinthians he spoke of the church being one body with many members. "God has so composed the body, giving the greater honor to the inferior part [those members regarded with less social esteem], that there may be no discord in the body, but that the members may have the same care for one another" (1 Corinthians 12:24, 25). In Galatians he declared his most famous line: "There is neither Jew nor Greek [no division based on social class], there is neither male nor female [no division based on sex]; for you are all one in Christ Jesus" (3:28). At Antioch, Paul stood up against Peter himself, who ate with Gentiles until a delegation of Jews from Jerusalem entered the place; then he quietly slipped away from the Gentiles so as not to be accused of being with them. Because of his influence, Barnabas and other Jews did the same. Watching from the sidelines, Paul saw what happened and publicly called Peter a hypocrite (see Galatians 2:11-14).

However, such teachings were not readily accepted but rather led to his imprisonment. Upon finishing his third missionary journey, Paul returned to Jerusalem to give a report to "the brethren." Since he had not required Gentile Christians to observe Jewish circumcisional and ceremonial customs, church leaders urged Paul to purify himself and certain Jewish Christians, so as to avoid any criticism from the Jewish Christian community (see Acts 21:20-24). Paul purified himself and those with him, and at the end of the required seven days of purification he went to the temple to give notice of the end of his purification and pay the necessary offering (verse 26). However, when a group of Jews from Asia saw him there, they incited a riot.

The riot was triggered by a rumor that Paul had brought an Ephesian named Trophimus into the temple, beyond the stone wall that separated the court of the Gentiles from the inner temple. An inscription in Latin and Greek (the languages of the Gentiles) warned foreigners not to trespass on penalty of death. Though it was only a rumor (verse 29), the feelings of racial hatred were so intense that "all the city was aroused" (verse 30). They seized Paul and dragged him out of the temple and were about to kill him, when the Roman commander charged with maintaining peace in the city rescued him. As he was being taken to prison, Paul asked the officer if he could speak to the crowd. Paul then gave his fellow Jews his personal testimony of a changed life and a converted attitude and action toward Gentiles (see Acts 22:1-21). The moment Paul began to include the salvation of the Gentiles in the mission of the church, the crowd turned on him again. At that point the commander rushed him off to prison (verse 24). Paul eventually appealed to Caesar and finally ended up in the Mamertine prison in Rome, from where he wrote words of encouragement to the Ephesians.

The Ephesians naturally felt devastated when they heard of Paul's imprisonment in Rome and very likely blamed themselves. After all, Paul was in prison because one of their number, Trophimus, had been accused of intrusion into the inner temple. Had it not been for that, Paul would still be free. Thus their state of anguish on seeing the one who brought them the gospel languishing in prison is understandable.

Paul wrote his letter to the Ephesians, not only to encourage them in their struggle, but also to help them understand God's purpose for His church, wherein there is no wall of racism between Jew and Gentile. Paul realized that this "dividing wall"—physically present in the temple, spiritually present in the church—had to come down before there could be unity in the church. And more important than the physical dividing wall was the mental, moral, and emotional dividing wall that would remain long after the physical wall was destroyed. Thus Paul wanted to show the Ephesians that through the church God would make manifest to the world the power of the gospel in bringing into existence a new humanity in Christ.

Paul knew that just as he was in prison, separated from social reality by incarcerating walls, so the church was held "captive" by social barriers—racial and sexual distinctions that separated members and kept them from experiencing the divine reality of oneness.

Thus the purpose of his letter was to "announce God's great plan, hidden from the beginning of the world, to create a messianic people of God, a new community of [people] uniting in Christ both Jew and Gentile and erasing the impenetrable social and religious barriers that had previously divided [humankind]."[4] This great plan is based on a whole new understanding of God, which moves the church from roles of dominance and dependence to compassion and loving concern.

Defining prejudice and racism

Before proceeding further, it is important to have in mind operating definitions of both *prejudice* and *racism*, as these will enable us better to understand the situation both in Paul's day and our own.

All of us tend to have prejudicial attitudes toward others. Such prejudice or "prejudgment" is often based on ignorance. It is a normal human response to racial, social, sexual, and other differences, since all human beings tend to prejudge others on the basis of limited knowledge, especially if others are different from themselves. Thus, we are all prejudiced and very few of us are exempt. In light of such a common human condition, the advice of my former seminary professor, Dr. Edward Heppenstall, is most helpful and worthy of practice: "The mark of a mature mind is the ability to suspend judgment until all the evidence is in."

What makes racial prejudice so sinister is not just the act of prejudging a person or a group. It is the act of prejudging another and then not changing one's mind even after receiving adequate evidence to the contrary, so that a person continues to *post*judge another in the same manner in which he *pre*judged. The old adage applies here: "A person convinced against his will is of the same opinion still." In the definition of prejudice, the indictment is greater for postjudgment than for prejudgment.

Prejudice is an attitude. When it results in an action, it becomes discrimination. Prejudice and discrimination combined form the basis for racism. However, racism is more than prejudice and discrimination. Racism is an *ideology. It is an ideology of supremacy that places a negative meaning on biological differences, resulting in an objective, differential, and unequal treatment.* Ideology is a system of ideas and beliefs about the universe to which people adhere in order to justify their attitudes and actions. Racism is both an attitude and an act of superiority that justifies its very existence by giving biological differences, such as skin color, texture of the hair, physical features, language, and cultural differences a negative meaning of inferiority. This negative meaning in turn legitimizes treating the other person as inferior to oneself. The result is an objective (visible, measurable, tangible) differential (there is an obvious difference between groups) and unequal treatment (treatment is not the same), where one group gets consistently shortchanged. The working definition for both racism and sexism is the same. Both refer to evil perpetrated against others. The only difference is that in racism, color is the excuse for oppression, while in sexism, it is gender. But racism has very little to do with color, just as sexism has little to do with sex or gender.

29

Biological differences are merely the excuse for oppression.

For example, no African or African-American person—or Hispanic or Asian or any person of dark skin color, for that matter—has ever suffered discrimination because of skin color, as much as this may surprise some. It is not skin color that forms the basis for discrimination, but the *negative meaning* given to the color of the skin.[5] "Color is neutral; it is the mind that gives it meaning."[6] Neither are women discriminated against because of their gender. Women are discriminated against because of the negative meaning given to their gender. Let me explain.

As human beings we have the capacity of giving meaning to the world around us. Take a piece of cloth, such as a white handkerchief. What is the function of a handkerchief? To wipe off sweat, clean our hands, wipe our mouths, blow our noses— all menial tasks. Is the meaning of these functions in the cloth? No. It is in culture, in our human society that has taught us to regard a handkerchief in this way. The same piece of cloth made into a shirt or blouse protects and celebrates our bodies. Add some red-and-blue cloth and a few stars, and the same cloth becomes a flag—the signature of a people, symbolizing their group identity or nationality. Many are willing to die for this cloth, to kill for it. Others will stand at attention with tears in their eyes in a moment of triumph, like the athletes at the Olympic Games when their national flag is raised in honor of their world-record victories.

Consider Karch Kiraly, captain of the United States Olympic volleyball team, which won the gold medal in both 1984 and 1988. The International Volleyball Federation has designated Kiraly "the world's best volleyball player." After his team won the gold medal at the 1984 games in Los Angeles, Kiraly declared, "I don't remember much about the last match for the gold in Los Angeles, and I don't remember the medal being put around my neck, but I'll never forget singing—screaming—the anthem as our flag went up just a little higher than the others."[7]

What did Kiraly scream for? For a mere piece of colored cloth! Not just any cloth, though, but a cloth imbued with meaning—a national symbol in which we all invest emotions.

The problem is that for too long, society has placed meaning, not just on cloth, but on its perception of physical characteristics such as skin color, hair texture, gender, age, religion, language, and social class. We have relegated some people to be the handkerchiefs of life and others to be the blouses and shirts, all the while securing a prominent place for those whom we chose to celebrate as flags. We even publish magazines and sleeze newspapers so that we can keep up with the daily life of our favorite human flags.

I submit to you that the United States is not only a multicultural nation, but also a nation in conflict with its values. For the meaning is not in the cloth or the gender or the hair. The meaning is neither in the color of a people's skin nor in their ethnic origin nor their language, but in the culture and in the social values transmitted from one generation to the next. This negative meaning, based on the belief that one group is superior to another, forms the basis for prejudice and discrimination, which result in racism in society and in the church.

Society's dominant forces have defined social roles that relegate people of color to inferior social positions. One of Christianity's most important tasks, therefore, is to counteract these negative class distinctions. This must be expressed in our worship and in our witness.

In American society we have a homogeneous value system operating within a heterogeneous society—our stereotypes and actions of discrimination dehumanize others, yet if we are all good enough for God, we ought to be good enough for each other.

This problem exists in the church as well. We tend to treat others, especially those who differ from us by race, class, or gender, as handkerchiefs—menial and insignificant, while we regard our colleagues and friends as shirts and blouses, and those in positions of power as flags before whom we do obeisance and pay our due respect.

Christianity begins with compassion—the ability to suffer with another to show loving, caring concern. The world needs

31

compassion, for compassion is a rare commodity in the social world market. There is a vast difference between sympathy and compassion. Sympathy *looks* down with teary-eyed pity and says, "I'm so sorry." Compassion *comes* down with caring concern and asks, "How can I help?" Sympathy stays in the realm of affection. Compassion always moves from affection to action. Compassion is the most basic principle in effective Christian practice, for it requires that we put ourselves in the place of another, and view life from the other's perspective, out of his or her context, out of his or her need, before we take any definitive action. That is why the Bible declares of Jesus, "When he saw the crowds, he had compassion for them, because they were harassed and helpless, like sheep without a shepherd" (Matthew 9:36). Jesus' very life was the personification of compassion.

Christianity thus begins with compassion—loving action that gives a positive meaning and sense of worth to all human beings. Each treats the other as the beautiful human flag that God created us all to be. Such action will enable our homes, our churches, our schools, our workplaces, our institutions, our communities, and our society to become strong at the broken places.

Racism has a material base

Racism is more than just a negative attitude toward others that arises out of prejudice. If that alone were the problem, then racism would be "reduced to something which takes place inside human heads, and the implicit presupposition here is that a change of attitude which will put an end to racial oppression can be brought about by dialogue, by an ethical appeal for a change of mentality."[8] However, such an understanding ignores two important considerations that lie at the root of racism—the material and moral basis of oppression.

Throughout human history racism has expressed itself in the socioeconomic exploitation of God's dark-skinned children. This has been justified by physical and biological differences, when the real reason was economic, as a result of competition. This material basis of exploitation is the principal reason be-

THE PROBLEM OF UNITY IN DIVERSITY

hind the white domination of the darker races—behind the
denial of the the dark races' access to power. The result has
been unequal treatment.

In 1903, W. B. E. DuBois, the great African-American
writer and sociologist, declared in his book, *The Souls of Black
Folk*, that "the problem of the twentieth century is the problem of the color-line—the relation of the darker to the lighter
races of men in Asia and Africa, in America and the islands of
the sea." Fifty years later however, he altered his views with
the realization that the real problems were economic, due to
"the fact that some civilized persons are willing to live in comfort even if the price of this is poverty, ignorance and disease
of the majority of their fellowmen."[9]

In order to justify such evil, people will appeal to that
which gives them a sense of meaning and ultimate value in
life—the ideological belief system that serves as the highest
authority in their lives, the moral basis of their existence.
Thus, if a person uses religion to explain social reality, that
person will use a religious ideology with its sacred writings to
justify this exploitation, thereby making the Divine the biggest exploiter of all. If, however, a scientific perspective dominates a person's worldview, then he will use a scientific ideology to show why some groups are inferior to others. The result is the same either way—the relegation of a segment of
God's creation to a second-class status and unequal treatment.

Racism is a moral issue

According to the gospel, racism is a moral issue and therefore a sin! James brings out this truth in chapter 2:8-11,
where he deals with class distinctions in the church as influenced by society.[10] The setting of chapter 2 is James's critique of the discriminating practice in his day of showing preferential treatment to the rich person attending the meetings
of the early Christians, in contrast to the low treatment ac-
corded the poor.

If a man with gold rings and in fine clothing comes into your
assembly, and a poor man in shabby clothing also comes in, and

33

3—B.W.

you pay attention to the one who wears the fine clothing and say, "Have a seat here, please," while you say to the poor man, "Stand there," or, "Sit at my feet," have you not made distinctions among yourselves, and become judges with evil thoughts? (verses 2-4).

James is admonishing the church to practice a principle of conduct based on the golden rule—what he calls "the royal law"—that says, "You shall love your neighbor as yourself" (verse 8). In verse 9 James declares, "If you show partiality, you commit sin, and are convicted by the law as transgressors." The expression *to show partiality* (from the Greek *prosopolemptéo*) means to "lift the face." It signifies an ancient custom, still prevalent in many societies, of lifting the face of the person who has entered the presence of another and bowed before him in humble greeting. The act of lifting the face signified an acknowledgement of the lower person's presence. It was a show of respect for that person.[11] The term meant to show respect for some people but not for others. *Prosopolemptéo*, "to show partiality," was a uniquely Christian expression, "found only in Christian writers."[12] The gospel of Jesus Christ challenges these discriminatory practices in society that tend to creep into the church. What else is racism, or sexism, if not a showing of partiality? James calls such action sin, and a transgression of God's moral law. In verse 11 James equates partiality with the cardinal sins of adultery and murder. Throughout history, both church and society have punished people for committing the sins of murder and adultery, but seldom if ever for the sins of racism and sexism—the showing of partiality. Yet for James, those who falter in this area are as guilty as if they had transgressed all of the law. "Whoever keeps the whole law but fails in one point has become guilty of all of it" (verse 10). Such a position was a reiteration of an Old Testament view: "He who despises his neighbor is a sinner" (Proverbs 14:21).

In verse 12 James goes on to declare, "So speak and so act as those who are to be judged under the law of liberty." What "law of liberty"? The moral law of God that liberates us from racism, sexism, and classism—"Love your neighbor as yourself" (verse 8). On these, Jesus declared, "depend all the law and the prophets (Matthew 22:40)—everything!

Sin has a social dimension

The view that racism is a moral issue and therefore sin, is based on a broader biblical understanding of sin not only as personal wrongdoing, but also as a social infraction of God's holy law. This is how Jesus and the Old Testament prophets viewed sin. Our problem is that we have been influenced by a Euro-American theology, arising out of a Western preoccupation with the individual, and this, in turn, has given rise to a privatized form of spirituality that sees religion exclusively from the personal dimension at the expense of the social. Rosemary Radford Ruether makes a most important point here:

> The apostasy of Christianity lies in its privatization and spiritualization. Privatization means one can be converted to God without being converted to each other. Spiritualization means one can declare that the Christ-nature is realized inwardly without having to deal with the contradictions of an unregenerate world.[13]

In Amos 2:6, 7, God, in the same breath, condemns both personal and social sins: "Thus says the Lord: 'For three transgressions of Israel, and for four, I will not revoke the punishment; because they sell the righteous for silver, and the needy for a pair of shoes—they that trample the head of the poor into the dust of the earth, and turn aside the way of the afflicted; a man and his father go in to the same maiden, so that my holy name is profaned.' " Here we have two different sins, one social—economic injustice against the poor; the other personal—illicit sexual conduct by both father and son. God condemns both equally as acts profaning the holy name of God. Yet throughout the history of the church, the emphasis of preachers has been more on sins of the flesh, such as sexual immorality, than on sins of injustice and economic oppression

35

of the poor. To God, both sins are equally grievous.

Failure to see sin in its social dimension leads many a good person to think that human injustice falls outside of his or her area of responsibility. "Our job is to save souls and not become involved in social issues," many declare. In saying this they fail to realize that social sin, as opposed to personal sin, is *transgenerational*—it "continues across generations. It is historically inherited. It is social sins that God has in mind when the Bible speaks of placing 'the [sins] of the fathers upon the children to the third and the fourth generation' (Exodus 20:5). Individuals are socialized into roles of domination and oppression and taught that these are normal and right. Discovery that the social system of which one is a part is engaged in chronic duplicity and contradiction, then, comes as a shock and an awakening. One has to reevaluate not only the social system, but one's own life in it; and not only what he has actually 'done,' but even more, what he has accepted from it."[14]

In Jesus', and Paul's day the Jews, as a religious people, possessed a theological worldview that led them to believe themselves better than anyone else, and they naturally appealed to their moral understanding of God for the way they structured their society with its racial, sexual, and social divisions. Such an approach is still in use today, for racism, like sexism, is based on the myth of the biological superiority of one group over another, and "myths are created to fill psychological needs."[15] This being the case, racism and sexism will persist in human hearts as long as they satisfy the felt needs of people—such as the need to feel superior to others.[16] "No amount of statistical data or hard scientific evidence suggesting a sociological rather than a genetic origin of differences will change a 'true believer's mythic ways."[17] Except the gospel.

Key themes

Paul's purpose in Ephesians was to bring about a change in this theological worldview by giving both Jew and Gentile not only a new understanding of God, but insight into God's great plan for all of humankind, and especially God's plan for the church. The letter begins with a profound statement of thanksgiving and praise to God for what He has done and what He proposes to do for His people. It is a statement of our spiritual heritage as sons and daughters of the Most High God (1:3-11). In the next three chapters, the rich insights in this portion of the letter will be unfolded, but for now I want to focus on four key words in the salutation, all of which are key themes throughout the letter.[18]

1. "By the will of God." Ephesians contains six references to God's will (chapter 1:1, 5, 9, 11; 5:17; 6:6)—more than any other epistle. This underlines a dominant theme in Ephesians: God's eternal will and plan to create a community of all people in Christ.

2. "To the saints," the holy ones. The term *holy* is used fourteen times in Ephesians—more than in any other letter except Romans, which is, of course, much longer. Ephesians emphasizes the continuity of God's holy people in the Old Testament, now broadened to include the Gentiles.

3. "Grace to you and peace." A most common greeting, the word *peace* is found seven times in Ephesians, again, more than in any other epistle except Romans. It announces a most basic theme of Ephesians, the possibility of peaceful unity and harmony among all humans through Christ.

4. "From God our Father." The concept of God as Father is used eleven times in Ephesians, once again more than in any other epistle except Romans. Ephesians brings forth a new understanding of God as the common source of the human family, which results in a new understanding of the church and of humanity.

What is this church like in which Jew and Gentile are made one? We can be sure that it is not a church where Gentiles are incorporated into Judaism, like synagogue proselytes. Nor, on the other hand, is it one where Christian Jews abandon the promises God gave to their fathers. Rather, the church is God's new creation, and Christians are a "third race"[19]—a new option among humanity. They are neither Jew nor Greek, but a new humanity in Christ; neither a White church nor a Black church, but a new creation in Christ; neither a White conference nor a Black conference, but a new structure reflective of Christ. These new structures result from a new under-standing of God, as the one Source from whom proceed the nations of the earth (Ephesians 3:14, 15).

These are the basic themes of Ephesians—themes that will be more fully explored later on. But the central theme of this letter is God's desire and plan to create a new humanity in Christ that knows no divisions, whether by attitude, action, or spirit; and out of which plan, the Christian church has come into existence, and that existence comprises its mission.

---

1. The "prison principle" and the bell curve that illustrates it are an adaptation of the Peter principle on which they build. See Laurence J. Peter and Raymond Hull, *The Peter Principle* (New York: Bantam Books, 1969), p. 28.

2. *Ibid.*

3. Joseph A. Grassi, "The Letter to the Ephesians," in *The Jerome Biblical Commentary*, edited by Raymond E. Brown, Joseph A. Fitzmyer, and Roland E. Murphy (Englewood Cliffs, N.J.: Prentice-Hall, Inc., 1968), p. 343.

4. *Ibid.*

5. Virtually all cultures give the color black a negative meaning, symbolic of evil and death. See F. M. Adams and C. E. Osgood, "A Cross-Cultural Study of the Affective Meanings of Color," *Journal of Cross-Cultural Psychology* 4 (1975), pp. 135-156. Cf. Mark G. Frank and Thomas Gilovich, "The Dark Side of Self- and Social Perception: Black Uniforms and Aggression in Professional Sports," *Journal of Personality and Social Psychology* 54:1(1988), pp. 74-85, and the special issue of *Daedalus, Journal of the American Academy of Arts and Sciences* (Spring 1967), on "Color and Race."

6. Roger Bastide, "Color, Racism, and Christianity," *Daedalus, Journal of the American Academy of Arts and Sciences* (Spring 1967), p. 312.

7. Peter Jensen, "Along the Way/Summer Olympics: The Athletes to Watch in Seoul," *Vis a Vis*, the Magazine of United Airlines, Inc., 2:9 (September 1988), p. 23.

8. Theo Witvliet, *A Place in the Sun: An Introduction to Liberation Theology in the Third World* (Maryknoll, N.Y.: Orbis Books, 1985), p. 45.

9. W. E. B. DuBois, "Fifty Years After," in *The Souls of Black Folk* (Greenwich, Conn.: Fawcett Publications, Inc., 1961), p. 14.

10. For an excellent study of this approach to the book of James, see Pedrito Maynard-Reid, *Poverty and Wealth in James* (Maryknoll, N.Y.: Orbis Books, 1987).

11. See E. Tiedtke, "Face," in *The New International Dictionary of New Testament Theology*, edited by Colin Brown (Grand Rapids, Mich.: Zondervan, 1975), vol. 1, p. 587.

12. W. F. Arndt and F. W. Gingrich, *A Greek-English Lexicion of the New Testament and Other Early Christian Literature* (Chicago: University of Chicago Press, 1957), p. 728. Cf. James H. Moulton and George Milligan, *The Vocabulary of the Greek Testament* (Grand Rapids, Mich.: Wm. B. Eerdmans, 1963), p. 553.

13. Rosemary Radford Ruether, "Rich Nations/Poor Nations: Towards a Just World Order in the Era of Neo-Colonialism," in *Christian Spirituality in the United States: Independence and Interdependence*, edited by Francis A. Figo, proceedings of the Theology Institute of Villanova University (Villanova, Penn.: Villanova University Press, 1978), pp. 82, 83.

14. Rosemary Radford Ruether, "Social Sin," *Commonweal* (January 30, 1981), p. 46.

15. Ashley Montague, *Man's Most Dangerous Myth: The Fallacy of Race*, 4th ed. (New York, 1965), p. 316.

16. Cited by Francis M. Wilhoit, *The Politics of Massive Resistance* (New York: George Braziller, 1973), p. 62.

17. *Ibid.*

18. See Grassi, p. 343.

19. Henry Chadwick, "Ephesians," *Peake's Commentary on the Bible*, edited by Matthew Black and H. H. Rowley (London: Thomas Nelson and Sons, Ltd., 1962), p. 980.

CHAPTER
Three

The Heavenly Status of Those Who Are in Christ

How should Christians resolve the problems that divide them? What procedures should they use? Who should lead out in the resolution of these problems? Ephesians and the stories of the New Testament provide us with significant insight into the answers to these questions. The solution that the early church developed to settle the conflict between Jewish and Greek Christians is particularly useful in this regard.

The first converts to Christianity were Jews of two types: Hellenistic and Palestinian[1] (the Palestinian Jews were also called Hebrews). The Hellenists were Jews of the Diaspora who lived throughout the Roman Empire outside of Palestine. They were more influenced by Greek culture (*Hellen* being the word for *Greek*) and often could speak only Greek, not Hebrew.[2] The Galileans were included in this group. All of these heard the gospel at Pentecost and accepted the Christian message (see Acts 2:5-11).

The Palestinian Jews, on the other hand, considered themselves to be the pure Israelites and discriminated against the Hellenists for moving away, not only from Palestine, but more importantly, from Jewish traditions, and for coming under foreign influence. Their situation was similar to that of first-generation Hispanics and Asians today, who have conflict with second-generation Hispanics and Asians for not being able to communicate in their native language, and who are regarded as being more American than Hispanic or Asian, having retained little of the Hispanic or Asian culture and way of life. This experience is common to most second-generation people in a foreign country.

For a time the impact of the gospel broke across all social barriers and brought about unity in Christian love. "Despite former prejudices, all were in harmony with one another." [3] The gospel of Jesus Christ, as an effective agent of change, was able to bring about harmony where there had been dissonance, unity where there had been schism, and understanding where there had been prejudice.

However, as the new believers became comfortable in their new environment and their experience of fellowship in Christ became more of a routine, they gradually reverted back to their old prejudices. Ellen White describes it this way:

> Satan knew that so long as this union continued to exist, he would be powerless to check the progress of gospel truth; and he sought to take advantage of former habits of thought, in the hope that thereby he might be able to introduce into the church elements of disunion. [4]

As a result of old differences, the Hebrews began behaving prejudicially toward the Hellenists. The situation finally came to a head in the economic program of distribution initiated by the early church to take care of the needy in their midst. The Hellenists complained that in the daily distribution the Hebrews were neglecting needy Hellenists, especially the widows (see Acts 6:1, 2). As stated in the last chapter, problems of prejudice and racism tend to have an economic basis. This has been a major problem in group conflict down through the ages. The early church's solution to the problem serves not only as a model in handling institutional inequities, but also provides us with a sound principle of group conflict resolution that our present-day church and society have yet to implement.

The structural solution to an age-old problem

Faced with this concern from the Hellenists, the leaders of the fledgling church did not head back to their tents to retrench themselves in their old positions. They analyzed the need, saw it as legitimate, and brought about structural change.

We should never see group conflict as a problem, but as an opportunity to do that which is just and right, in harmony with the gospel. Obviously, the more ethnically diverse a group is, the greater the possibility for tension and conflict. Sociologist Lewis Coser declares that "the greater the structural or cultural diversity of those who unite in a coalition, the more their interests other than in the immediate purpose are likely to be divergent if not antagonistic. Such a coalition, if it is not to fall apart, must attempt to keep close to the purposes for which it was formed."[5] Groups differ in their interests and needs. The more cultural these differences are, the greater will be the potential for antagonism within the group. This is why the McGavran School of Church Growth advocates the "homogeneous unit" principle: "Men like to become Christians without crossing racial, linguistic, or class barriers."[6] It is true that a homogeneous group, in terms of race, culture, and class, will experience less conflict. However, the gospel does not save people *in* their sins, but *from* their sins of segregation, division, and exclusiveness. The dividing wall of ethnic/racial hostility that Jesus broke down, but that society still maintains, must not be erected in the church.

When a group loses sight of its mission, its members will turn on each other by focusing on their differences, especially if the group is culturally diverse. Such was the problem in the early church between Hebrew and Hellenist. Though both groups were comprised of Jews, they were culturally diverse. The social program of "daily distribution," which met the material needs of the members, began taking precedence over the church's spiritual mission. Any time the gospel's social and spiritual dimensions are out of balance, the stage is set

42

for group conflict, especially if one group is neglected. A culturally pluralistic group needs to maintain a clear focus on the purpose for which it was formed. Otherwise, the factors that tend to divide it will assume greater importance than the factors that unite it.

However, group tension especially between ethnic groups, should be regarded positively rather than negatively. Tension is like one's pulse: if it is visible through the skin, it is a sign that the body is sick; if it is absent, the body is dead; however, if it is present but not visible through the skin, it is a sign of health. The same is true of tension in an organization. When it is either throbbing or absent, the organization is being defeated by conflict or else it is "dead"—not going anywhere. However, when creative tension is present but concealed, an organization experiences dynamic growth.

The apostles acted in accordance with the gospel, and the result was a proper division of labor. It is important to notice who was placed into positions of leadership: the Hellenists themselves. All seven persons chosen were Hellenists, for they all had Greek names. In other words, leaders were chosen from the very group that was objecting to structural inequity, to oversee the work of distribution not only for the Greek widows, but also for the entire church body. What an amazing strategy! And it was based on an important principle of group relations: We should listen carefully to those who are closest to a problem and where possible select persons from the group to lead out in its resolution. This was the lesson that the United States as a nation was forced to learn on that fateful day, January 28, 1986, when the entire nation saw the space shuttle *Challenger* explode on takeoff with seven passengers aboard. The lesson is this: *Failure to listen to those who are closest to a problem may result in the whole system exploding in our face.*

Often those in power declare, "We cannot turn leadership over to others or the program will fail." What a narrow-minded thought! The success of most programs does not depend on any one person or group. We must never forget that God is the Head of the church.

This restructuring of labor to preserve unity resulted in an immediate increase in the number of converts to Christ. Prior to the restructuring, the Lord "*added* to their number day by day those who were being saved" (Acts 2:47). But after the restructuring the Bible declares that "the word of God increased; and the number of the disciples *multiplied* greatly in Jerusalem, and a great many of the priests were obedient to the faith" (Acts 6:7). What amazing results! Who were these priests that were now "obedient to the faith"? They were the very ones that gave Jesus such a hard time during His ministry. Now, when they saw how the gospel removed prejudice, they joined.

Unfortunately, even though the leaders of the early church responded to the charge of discrimination with a positive structural change, Jewish hatred for the Roman oppressor and for anyone not of their race and faith strongly influenced the behavior of Jewish Christians, so that even though many believed one thing, they sometimes practiced another. An example was Peter's experience in Antioch (see Galatians 2:11-14).

Saint Peter's sin

If anyone should have had a change in attitude and action toward Gentiles, it was Peter, as a result of his experience with Cornelius (see Acts 10). Unfortunately, his behavior in refusing to continue eating with Gentile Christians in the presence of a Jewish delegation from Jerusalem forced Paul to rebuke him. Paul told Peter that his behavior was hypocritical and not in a straight line (Greek: *orthopodeo*—to walk in a straight line) with the truth of the gospel (see Galatians 2:13, 14). Thus, the sin of Saint Peter—racial and ethnic segregation and preferential treatment—has become the sin of the church, dividing it along racial and economic lines.

Why did Paul have a different attitude toward Gentiles than Peter, in spite of the fact that Peter had received a special revelation from God on the matter? One possible answer may be that Peter was a Palestinian Jew, whereas Paul was a Hellenistic Jew, born and reared in Tarsus, the capital of Cilicia (present-day Turkey). Though Peter was from Bethsaida, a multiracial community on the northeastern shore of the Sea of Galilee,[7] Jews were still in the majority and tended to keep themselves separate from the foreign population. Paul, on the other hand, lived in an integrated community where Jews were in the minority. He was a Roman citizen by birth and a Jew by ancestry, but above all a son of God by spiritual adoption. Such a situation gave him a different attitude toward Gentiles and enabled him to minister effectively in the real world of a multicultural society. Thus, Paul was able to accomplish much more than Peter because he was part of the world in which he lived and not isolated from it.

The context of Ephesians

As Paul reflects on the events leading to his present status—"a prisoner for Christ"—he realizes that, because of the situation with Trophimus, the Ephesians might blame themselves for his imprisonment. The Ephesians loved Paul dearly. He spent more time at Ephesus than at any of the other churches he established—some three years (see Acts 19:1-20; 20:31).

No longer the worker, but now the prisoner, Paul writes to encourage the Ephesians in their faith, but more importantly, to give them a broad understanding of how God views the universal church (and not just the situation in Ephesus). The central theme of his letter is unity in the church—unity in diversity in Christ. It is God's intention to create one new humanity in Christ so that the dividing walls of racial and ethnic separation that segregate the world may not exist in the church. Each Christian is to manifest this new oneness in all areas of life. This is the overriding theme of Ephesians, and every section of the letter needs to be understood against this thematic backdrop.

The hymn of praise

The opening section of Ephesians (chapter 1:3-14) is a hymn of praise and thanksgiving for God's blessings. Picture, if you will, a difficult jigsaw puzzle with many intricate pieces.

In order to know how to put it together, we need the cover picture that gives an overview of what the final product will look like.

This opening hymn of praise and thanksgiving is that cover picture. It portrays the beautiful spiritual inheritance that is in store for all who love God. Notice how clearly the Phillips translation of the passage sets forth the promised blessings:

Praise be to God for giving us through Christ every possible spiritual benefit as citizens of Heaven! For consider what he has done—before the foundation of the world he chose us to become, in Christ, his holy and blameless children living within his constant care. He planned, in his purpose of love, that we should be adopted as his own children through Jesus Christ— that we might learn to praise that glorious generosity of his which has made us welcome in the everlasting love he bears toward the Son. It is through the Son, at the cost of his own blood, that we are redeemed, freely forgiven through that full and generous grace which has overflowed into our lives and opened our eyes to the truth. For God has allowed us to know the secret of his plan, and it is this: he purposes in his sovereign will that all human history shall be consummated in Christ, that everything that exists in Heaven or earth shall find its perfection and fulfillment in him. And here is the staggering thing—that in all which will one day belong to him we have been promised a share (since we were long ago destined for this by the one who achieves his purposes by his sovereign will), so that we, as the first to put our confidence in Christ, may bring praise to his glory! And you too trusted him, when you had heard the message of truth, the Gospel of your salvation. And after you gave your confidence to him you were, so to speak, stamped with the promised Holy Spirit as a guarantee of purchase, until the day when God completes the redemption of what he has paid for as his own; and that will again be to the praise of his glory.

Now that is something to get excited about! It is so beautiful, so vast, so all-encompassing, that we cannot do it justice with a mere casual reading. The hymn divides easily into three sections. Verses 3-6 portray the heavenly status of those who are in Christ. Paul shows us here that the church's origin is rooted in eternity, and the source of our salvation resides in God's love. The second section (verses 7-10) shows that this love is manifested in Christ's work on our behalf, through whom the mystery of God is revealed. And what is this "mystery"? It is God's plan to unite the nations as one in Christ. The third section (verses 11-14), shows how God plans to create one new humanity that includes both Jew and Gentile. The guarantee of the success of this plan is the impartation of the Holy Spirit, which is the down payment of our eternal inheritance.

The status of those who are in Christ

The hymn begins with a blessing pronounced on God: "Blessed be the God and Father of our Lord Jesus Christ" (Ephesians 1:3). How is it possible for humans to bless God, when the usual procedure is the other way around? Most blessings come from the older and wiser to the younger. It should be God who blesses humans. In Hispanic culture, for example, it is the practice of children, even after marriage, to ask their parents for a blessing—a *bendición*—especially if they have not seen or spoken to them in a while. So how is it that humans can bless God? We "bless" God by not forgetting His benefits, by recounting how He has blessed us. Psalm 103:1, 2, declares:

> Bless the Lord, O my soul;
> and all that is within me, bless his holy name!
> Bless the Lord, O my soul,
> and forget not all his benefits.

And what are these benefits? Verses 3 to 5 list them:

> Who forgives all your iniquity,
> who heals all your diseases,
> who redeems your life from the Pit,
> who crowns you with steadfast love and mercy,

47

who satisfies you with good as long as you live
so that your youth is renewed like the eagle's.

We can "bless" God only in thanksgiving of heart and voice as we rejoice over His works on our behalf. The natural question of the appreciative soul is found in Psalm 116:12: "What shall I render to the Lord for all his bounty to me?" And the immediate response is, "I will lift up the cup of salvation and call on the name of the Lord" (verse 13).

We find this very same thought in Ephesians. God is to be blessed—for what? For blessing "us in Christ with every spiritual blessing in the heavenly places" (chap. 1:3). Notice the all-inclusiveness of the text—"*every* spiritual blessing in the heavenly places." That is, with every blessing that can be found in heaven. That's like saying, "Go ahead and write a check. All the gold in Fort Knox is yours to back it up!" That would be some blessing! Except that in reality Fort Knox is bankrupt compared with the reserve of blessings God has in store for us in "Fort Heaven," completely at our disposal.

Yet these blessings are not available to just anyone. Just as you can't walk into Fort Knox and take out gold unless you have government security clearance, so not everyone is able to draw out these "spiritual blessings" from Fort Heaven. Who can, then? Only those, Paul says, who are "in Christ." That expression is used more than thirty times in this letter alone, making it clear that the medium through which God, as the Source of every good, does anything for human beings, is our Lord Jesus Christ. "Praise be to God for giving us through Christ every possible spiritual benefit as citizens of Heaven!" (verse 3, Phillips).

What are these spiritual blessings? Here Paul lifts up the cup of salvation and recounts the plan of redemption:

> Consider what he has done—before the foundation of the
> world he chose us to become, in Christ, his holy and blameless
> children living within his constant care. He planned, in his pur-
> pose of love, that we should be adopted as his own children
> through Jesus Christ—that we might learn to praise that

glorious generosity of his which has made us welcome in the everlasting love he bears toward the Son (verses 4-6, Phillips).

Our salvation is no accident. The divine choice to save humanity has been part of God's plan from the beginning. "The plan for our redemption was not an afterthought, a plan formulated after the fall of Adam."[8] God did not find Himself caught up short by sin, in a state of despair, wringing His hands and wondering what to do when His precious children rebelled against Him. Our salvation has its roots in eternity. We are not the result of some biological process of natural selection, devoid of purpose and meaning. Neither are we the result of some cosmic explosion. No! We are the result of a divinely constructed plan that has purpose, meaning, and direction. We know where we are going because we know where we came from. Thus, the origin of the church is rooted in eternity.

The racial chaos experienced by the early church, which is still present in the church today, was the result of the failure of God's people to understand His eternal plan for all humanity. Through Christ, God desires to create a new community, comprised of new men and new women, new boys and new girls—a new humanity—with no divisions of any type, under the Lordship of one corporate Head, Jesus Christ.

In view of this plan, Paul declares that we are to be "holy and blameless before him" (verse 4)—terms ·from the Old Testament sacrificial offerings that he now applies to the living offering of Christians uniting themselves to Christ (see Romans 12:1, 2). Paul means that Christians cannot continue discriminating against each other and still call themselves "holy and blameless before God." In other words, we cannot continue to harbor ethnocentric feelings—each one thinking that his/her group is "the center of everything, and all others are scaled and rated with reference to it"[9]—and be blameless. The blamelessness Paul speaks of in Ephesians refers primarily to the relationship God wants His people to have with each other in order to bring about a new community in Christ. It is therefore a blamelessness having to do with social sin, and not primarily with personal sin. Though personal sin is included, it is only secondary and not primary in the text.

Christians need to reread the Bible, not through the eyes of Western individualism, but through the sociological eye of the Hebrews and their prevailing understanding of God's actions in the world from the perspective of the corporate community. To the Hebrew, the individual is never in isolation, as in American society. Our individualism results in a great deal of personal alienation with a sense of hopelessness and meaninglessness. Hebrew thinking places the individual as an integral part of the community. The individual thus has a corporate personality that links the person to the community.[10]

This is the meaning behind verse 5: "He destined us in love to be his sons through Jesus Christ, according to the purpose of his will." We are adopted into God's family of the redeemed. It is not a question of individual salvation, but of salvation within a community, a select sister/brotherhood of daughters and sons saved through Christ. This was God's purpose all along because of His love for Jesus Christ. Our salvation resides in God's love for Christ, and through Christ for us. This is what Jesus declared in His prayer in John 17: " 'I in them and thou in me, that they may become perfectly one, so that the world may know that thou hast loved them even as thou hast loved me' " (verse 23). In the next verse, Jesus tells us that God's love for Him was "before the foundation of the world" (verse 24). Since He is our "Elder Brother," we come riding in on our Brother's coattails. Salvation comes to the believer in and through a community in Christ—the community of the redeemed incorporated in Christ.

This is the heavenly status of those who are in Christ. We are incorporated into the family of God through divine adoption as sons and daughters of God. The implication of this truth of our interhuman relations is most profound. On earth our social status often is lowly. Think of the status that Gentile Christians had among Jewish Christians in Paul's day. In our day, think of the status of Black South Africans in South Africa. Think of the status of African-Americans in the United States, of the millions of refugees, the displaced peoples of the earth, and their lack of status here on earth. Think of the countless homeless, both in the affluent urban centers of the "First World" and in the hovels of the sprawling cities of the Third World—cities such as Caracas, Calcutta, and Cairo. None of these groups have any status. As Martin Luther King used to say, "If color made them different, misery and oppression made them the same."[11] But in Christ they have the highest possible status: *sons and daughters of God.*

However, the fact that our status is high in Christ does not mean that we do nothing about social situations here on earth. That is precisely the charge that Karl Marx brought against accommodating religion in his day: that Christians used their religion to oppress people while promising them a change of conditions in heaven someday. Such Christianity truly is "opium," as Marx called it, for it is "a drug" that desensitizes people to their miserable condition on earth. Communism developed from this heretical view of Christianity and became a powerful challenge to apostate Christianity. As long as the church continues practicing injustice, while telling people that their condition cannot be changed until Jesus comes, it will continue to be challenged by Communism, especially in the Third World, where oppression is most visible.

In view of this situation in our world today, we need to take the message to the Ephesians seriously. The divine status that all of God's children have in Christ is to be made a visible reality, in living color, in the corporate community of the redeemed—the church—which is the visible manifestation of God's new humanity in Christ. This must not happen at some time in the future, but now. It must become visible in the church today.

No wonder Paul closes this first section with a shout of praise! "To the praise of his glorious grace which he freely bestowed on us in the Beloved" (verse 6). This is a recurrent theme in Ephesians: Human beings, upon understanding God's plan, should praise Him and give Him thanks. Praise God!

---

1. See James D. G. Dunn, *Unity and Diversity in the New Testa-*

ment: An Inquiry Into the Character of Earliest Christianity (Philadelphia: The Westminster Press, 1977), p. 268, ff.

2. *Ibid.*, p. 268.

3. Ellen G. White, *The Acts of the Apostles* (Mountain View, Calif.: Pacific Press, 1911), p. 87.

4. *Ibid.*, pp. 87, 88.

5. Lewis Coser, *The Functions of Social Conflict* (New York: The Free Press, 1956), p. 144.

6. Donald McGavran, *Understanding Church Growth* (Grand Rapids, Mich.: Wm. B. Eerdmans, 1970), p. 198.

7. Cf. my article, "The Significance of Galilee," Lake Union *Ministerial Digest* 3:2 (Spring 1985).

8. Ellen G. White, *The Desire of Ages* (Mountain View, Calif.: Pacific Press, 1898), p. 22.

9. William Graham Sumner, *Folkways and Mores* (New York: Schocken Books, 1979), p. 13.

10. See H. Wheeler Robinson, *Corporate Personality in Ancient Israel*, Facet Books, Biblical Series—11 (Philadelphia: Fortress Press, 1964).

11. Martin Luther King, Jr., *Where Do We Go From Here: Chaos or Community?* (Boston: Beacon Press, 1967), p. vii.

CHAPTER

Four

The Unity of All in Christ

With the coming of Jesus Christ something glorious happened to the human family, and in Ephesians 1 Paul tells what it is: "In him we have redemption through his blood, the forgiveness of our trespasses, according to the riches of his grace which he lavished upon us" (verse 7). The phrases "Redemption through his blood" and "the forgiveness of our trespasses" summarize Christ's work on behalf of the human family. They are not identical, but complementary. The first, "Redemption through his blood," looks at Christ's saving work from God's side. The second, "Forgiveness of sins," views that work from the human side. Both are accomplished realities by One who is at once both the Son of God and the Son of humanity. "Together they represent the whole truth."[1]

Redemption and forgiveness

The primary idea of *redemption* is deliverance. "It implies setting free a person or group that is under someone else's power or in slavery.[2] It is used in the Old Testament to describe the deliverance of God's people from Egypt. In the New

Testament, God wants to redeem both Jew and Gentile. Both are in bondage to sin. But the word for *sin* or *trespasses* is not sin in the abstract, as some disembodied concept divorced from reality. Sin is always concrete and takes on personal and social dimensions. The word for *trespasses* in this text means "separate acts of transgression."[3]

The sin from which God redeemed the Israelites in Egypt was slavery—the sin of oppression. "Behold, the cry of the people of Israel has come to me, and I have seen the oppression with which the Egyptians oppress them." "I have seen the affliction of my people who are in Egypt, and have heard their cry because of their taskmasters; I know their sufferings, and I have come down to [redeem] them out of the hand of the Egyptians, and to bring them up out of that land" (Exodus 3:9, 7, 8). The redemption of the Israelites was real and tangible because the sin of the Egyptians was real and substantive, not abstract and nebulous.

We find the same in the New Testament between Jew and Gentile. The inward prejudice that the Jews held toward the Gentiles manifested itself in outward acts of discrimination, making it difficult for Gentiles to accept Christ. And even when they did, divisions were maintained, preserving distinction between the two. Thus, indifference manifested itself in "separate acts of transgression," as Paul declares.

Paul's point is that, as the Head and Representative of the human race, Jesus came to set both Jew and Gentile free from social bondage by offering Himself as the full and perfect sacrifice for sin. Christ thus offers both groups forgiveness through His blood, which makes at-one-ment, so that instead of two separate rivals, there is now one new humanity in Christ. But if both have accepted this redemption and forgiveness, how then can they continue with the same behavior *after* redemption that prevailed *before*? Such is behavior that lies behind prejudice, only now the indictment is greater, for "post-behavior" is much worse than "pre-behavior."

Lavished grace
This is why Paul told Peter that his behavior at Antioch was

hypocritical and contrary to the truth of the gospel. So is the present behavior of the church, if it persists in holding segregationist and racist attitudes toward the various members of the household of faith, making of two that which God at an unspeakable price has made into one! Never mind that society is doing it. Christians live by a different ethic because above and beyond being American, African, Asian, or Antillian, we are *adopted* sons and daughters of the living God, purchased by His blood, and one with the divine family! Therefore, Paul says, "In him *we* [Jew and Gentile, Black, White, Brown, Yellow] have redemption through his blood, the forgiveness of our trespasses, according to the riches of his grace which he lavished upon us" (Ephesians 1:7, emphasis supplied).

All this comes to us by grace—free, unmerited, undeserved, yet sufficient and overflowing. The word *abound* in the King James Version does not quite do justice in conveying the full meaning of the original. The word means "to lavish on to the point of overflowing." An illustration might clarify the meaning. Suppose you are a homeless beggar in the dead of winter on the windy streets of downtown Chicago, at the corner of State and Madison. You meet a holiday shopper and ask for a quarter, but you expect only a dime. Instead, he gives you a $100 bill, his warm winter overcoat, and his business card. Then he tells you that tomorrow he will take you home as his adopted son. As you stand there in a warm daze, he turns to leave, then looks back and says, "See you tomorrow. And by the way, merry Christmas." Merry Christmas? Hallelujah! That's grace—all-sufficient, overflowing, undeserved grace. It is also the redeeming gospel.

God has lavished on us so much grace that it overflows the soul, not only with salvation, but also with wisdom and insight. These gifts are important. *Wisdom* signifies "the knowledge of the true end of life," which comes only when we understand the divine purpose of God's will, while *insight* means "wise judgment" as to what our actions should be in the light of this knowledge about the divine purpose of God's will.[4] God's purpose is the mystery of His will. Paul uses the word *mystery* here as something that was hidden but is now re-

55

vealed in Christ. And what is this hidden thing—now revealed? It is God's purpose "to unite all things in [Christ]" (verse 10). In Ephesians, the mystery of God's will "means the hidden plan of God to create a universal community of human beings in Christ."[5] "In these words Paul strikes the great keynote of the whole letter, *the unity of all in Christ.*"[6]

Gathered in Christ

In order to fully grasp the meaning of the phrase "gathered in Christ" and its significance in God's total plan for humanity, we need to understand the meaning of the Greek *anakephalo*—"to unite." This word is used only twice in the New Testament: here and in Romans 13:9. It means "to gather together as one," "to sum up under one head." The verb "literally means to place at the top of a column the sum of figures that have been added."[7] The picture is one of a lot of scattered numbers that are difficult to add up to a total, but Christ gathers them together, lines them up, and writes the total at the top. In today's jargon we might say, "Get all your ducks in a row." In Romans 13:9 all the commandments are *summed up* in one: "Love your neighbor as yourself." Ephesians carries the additional thought that this gathering up is "in Christ."

Right here, in this central portion of the thanksgiving hymn, this picture-cover, lies the heart of the entire message to the Ephesians—the message that above all others the church is to believe, live, and preach. It is found in this phrase, "To unite all things in Christ." "The full meaning of this expression is 'to gather again under one head' things which had been originally one, but had since been separated."[8] Originally, the human family was one, but sin created a separation that distorts not only God's character but also the character of human beings. Humans, by their separation, no longer act like beings made in the image of God. Like random numbers, they are scattered, everyone thinking that he is more important than his neighbor, that his ethnic group is superior to all others. But Christ, who is the Head of all, through the incarnation and atonement, brings them together as one again.

The best statement of this truth is found in Colossians 1:15-20:

> He is the image of the invisible God, the first-born of all creation; for in him all things were created, in heaven and on earth, visible and invisible, whether thrones or dominions or principalities or authorities—all things were created through him and for him. He is before all things, and in him all things hold together. He is the head of the body, the church; he is the beginning, the first-born from the dead, that in everything he might be pre-eminent. For in him all the fulness of God was pleased to dwell, and through him to reconcile to himself all things, whether on earth or in heaven, making peace by the blood of his cross.

Alfred Barry declares:

> In Christ, as the word of God in the beginning, all created things are considered as gathered up, through Him actually made, and in Him continuing to exist. This unity, broken by sin, under the effect of which "all creation groans" (Romans 8:22), is restored in the Incarnation and Atonement of the Son of God.[9]

Herein lies the significance of Christianity: that the unity of the human family, broken by sin, under the effect of which "all creation groans," is restored in the incarnation and atonement of the Son of God. No wonder the Christian is to behave differently!

By this act, all things—things in heaven and things on earth, from the higher to the lower, from the greater to the lesser—are again summed up in Christ, and again made one in Him with God.

> In present-day terms we would say that God's purpose was to give a new hope to a world divided by barriers of race, color, culture, or political divisions and make possible a unity among humans through Christ. [Thus] Christ, the new Adam and the head of a new complete people of God, has been entrusted with

the mission of bringing the universe into a state of unity and harmony.[10]

However, Christ did not come to bring about this unity in the world, but in the church. And when the world sees this unity in the church, it will believe that Jesus Christ has come as Lord and Saviour. This was precisely Jesus' final prayer in John 17:23: "I in them and thou in me, that they may become perfectly one, so that the world may know that thou hast sent me and hast loved them even as thou hast loved me." Jesus refers, not so much to a theological unity, as this text is often understood, but to a sociological unity—a unity in actual practice. Unity of belief is not all that impressive, for the real test of the genuineness of a belief is not what people intellectually adhere to, but what they actually practice. Jesus is concerned about the *sociological* unity of the church, Black, White, and Brown together, without racial, social, or class distinction, as one family in the household of faith. This is the unity Jesus desired to see expressed in outward behavior, "That they may become perfectly one." For the lack of this oneness in the church, the world does not believe.

Therein lies the challenge to the church.

1. Alfred Barry, "The Epistle to the Ephesians," in *Ellicott's Commentary on the Whole Bible*, edited by Charles John Ellicott (Grand Rapids, Mich.: Zondervan Publishing House, 1970), p. 17.

2. Joseph A. Grassi, "The Letter to the Ephesians," in *The Jerome Biblical Commentary*, edited by Raymond E. Brown, Joseph A. Fitzmyer, and Roland E. Murphy (Englewood Cliffs, N.J.: Prentice-Hall, Inc., 1968), p. 343.

3. Barry, p. 17.

4. *Ibid*, p. 18.

5. Grassi, p. 344.

6. Barry, p. 18, emphasis supplied.

7. Grassi, p. 344.

8. Barry, p. 18.

9. *Ibid*.

10. Grassi, p. 344.

Five

Tomorrow Is Already Here

Paul's letter to the Ephesians dwells on the theme that while believers will experience the social divisions of racism, classism, and sexism in the world, in the church they are to experience oneness. This oneness is summarized in Galatians 3:28: "There is neither Jew nor Greek [no racism], there is neither slave nor free [no classism], there is neither male nor female [no sexism]; for you are all *one* in Christ Jesus" (emphasis supplied).

The hymn of praise that we have been considering in the last two chapters makes clear that this was God's plan for humanity before the foundation of the world, because in love He destined us to be united as one in Christ. In the last section of the hymn, Ephesians 1:11-14 (the subject matter of this chapter), Paul tells us who is included in this plan and what kind of guarantee God has given us of its fulfillment.

The plan includes everyone

In him, according to the purpose of him who accomplishes all things according to the counsel of his will, we who first hoped in Christ have been destined and appointed to live for the praise of his glory. In him you also, who have heard the word of truth, the gospel of your salvation, and have believed in him, were sealed with the promised Holy Spirit, which is the guarantee of our inheritance until we acquire possession of it, to the praise of his glory (verses 11-14).

Notice the progression of thought:
1. *"We* who first hoped."
2. *"You* also, who have heard the word."
3. "The guarantee of *our* inheritance."

Who are the *we*, the *you*, and the *our*? The *we* refers to the Jewish people—and Paul was a Jew. The Old Testament describes them as the inheritance of God (see Deuteronomy 32:9). To them the good news of salvation came first. Paul declared in Romans 9, "To them belong the sonship, the glory, the covenants, the giving of the law, the worship, and the promises; to them belong the patriarchs, and of their race, according to the flesh, is the Christ" (verses 4, 5). Jesus reinforced this by saying, "Salvation is from the Jews" (John 4:22). Therefore, it is "for the Jews first and also for the Gentiles" (Romans 2:9, TEV).

The *you* refers to the Gentiles, in this case the Ephesians, who also have placed their trust in Christ. Together, both Jew and Gentile comprise the "our," a new third group—the new humanity in Christ. This is what the power of the gospel does to the lines of ethnic divisions that so fragment our small planet into more than 200 nations, grouped under the sociopolitical-economic categories of "First World," "Second World," and "Third World." In Christ, such divisions melt away, for the gospel returns us to the oneness that the human family had with each other and with God in the beginning. The purpose of the gospel is to return us to the beginning. However, this won't be the same beginning, but a *new* beginning—one that now includes Jesus Christ as part of the human family. Because of this new dimension, the second beginning will be better then the original, for Immanuel is now with us!

This inheritance—this being one with God again—is the

divine purpose to which we have been predestined. In other words, God decided before the foundation of the world that we should be destined for glory, that we should be "in Christ." God has not destined anyone to be lost, to be damned to hell. No! Any such destiny is of our own choosing. It is never God's choice. His choice is different. Paul tells us that "the purpose of him who accomplishes all things according to the counsel of his will" is, for us, to be found "in Christ," living "for the praise of his glory" (Ephesians 2:11, 12). How do we live "for the praise of his glory"? By manifesting in all our relationships that unity in Christ that transcends the earthly, social barriers of race, color, and culture that bring economic and political divisions. Such action, unheard of and unseen in the world, brings praise to God's glory.

The sealing of the Spirit

How is such action possible? Paul explains the simple, three-step process in verse 13:

1. We must first hear the word of truth, the gospel of our salvation.

2. We must believe in Christ.

3. We are then sealed with the promised Holy Spirit.

It is as simple as one-two-three: Hear, believe, be sealed.

Hear what? The word of truth—the gospel of our salvation—that through the saving work of Christ, His redeeming sacrifice grants us forgiveness of personal and social sin so that people of all nations stand before God as one family in Him. It was this "truth of the gospel" that Peter denied by his hypocritical action in Antioch (see Galatians 2:11-14).

But more than hearing is involved. We must also believe in Christ. We must place our complete trust in Him. And the result of that trust is that we are "sealed' with the Holy Spirit.

What is this *sealing*? Such an expression might sound strange to us because it involves a practice no longer used today with the same meaning as in ancient times. Today we have contracts, stamps, Scotch tape, staplers, self-adhesive folders, insurance, etc., all to guarantee ownership, protection, and security of goods.

In ancient times, when seals were most common, a seal meant several things. It was a mark of ownership. The item so sealed belonged to the owner of the seal. It proved to whom the item belonged. A seal also served as a means of protection, for all sealed goods were protected. The religious leaders asked Pilate to seal the tomb so that no one could steal the body of Christ (see Matthew 27:62-66). The seal also guaranteed against violation. That which was sealed could not be opened. Finally, a seal served as an accreditation. It ensured that the content was credible, that it was what it claimed to be. In other words, it ensured against fraud.

All of these traits are included in the sealing of the Holy Spirit. Those who have heard the truth of the gospel and have believed in Christ are sealed with the promised Holy Spirit. The sealing of the Holy Spirit is a mark of ownership. The Christian belongs to God. The identity of the Christian is thus clear. God's seal is also a protection, for Satan cannot touch us (see Isaiah 43:1-7; John 10:27-30). He cannot jeopardize God's plan for us (see Romans 8:28). The sealing of the Holy Spirit also guarantees against violation. This will be especially meaningful to God's people at the end of time, when the final sealing of God's people takes place, shortly before a death decree is issued (see Revelation 13:15). The seal of God at that time will protect God's people from any violation that might result in their physical annihilation. It also serves as a guarantee that God's people are genuine, that they are who God says they are.

But the seal mentioned in Ephesians 1 adds one more important point: It guarantees the certainty of our final salvation (verse 14). In other words, our salvation is sure. The plan to bring about unity in the family of God is guaranteed, and God will have a people—that new humanity in Christ—who fully and visibly reflect God's purposes for the human race.

Alfred Barry declares that "in this passage the very title given to the Spirit is significant. He is called (in the curious order of the original), 'The Spirit of the Promise, the Holy One.' 'The promise' is clearly the promise in the Old Testament (see Jeremiah 31:31-34; Joel 2:28-32) of the outpouring of the Spirit on all God's people in 'the latter days.' The emphatic position of the title 'Holy One' seems to point to the effect of His indwelling in the actual sanctification of the soul thus sealed."[1]

This sealing takes place at baptism. "Devotees of various pagan gods sometimes branded themselves with the name of the deity to whom they belonged and by whom they were protected. Baptism through the Spirit is the visible sign of incorporation into Christ."[2] It becomes the seal of our conversion (see Acts 2:38). In 2 Corinthians 1:22 Paul says that God "has put his seal upon us and given us his Spirit in our hearts as a guarantee." A guarantee of what? In Ephesians 1:14 he gives the answer: "The guarantee of our inheritance until we acquire possession of it, to the praise of his glory."

Thus, "the link between this life and the salvation to come is the seal of the Spirit given as a 'guarantee,' the first installment of which promises future payment in full."[3] The Greek word for *guarantee* (KJV—*earnest*) is *arrabon*, which is taken from the trader's market. It is "a down payment to guarantee full payment."[4]

Conclusion

This passage tells us that "tomorrow, though it remain tomorrow, is already here."[5] Our salvation is so guaranteed that we have nothing to fear for the future, for the future is now. Our future inheritance with Christ is already a present, living reality. We have it in our possession. We are saved—and that to the praise of His glory!

But this certainty is only guaranteed to those who have heard the truth of the gospel, who have believed in Christ, and who have received the seal of the Holy Spirit at baptism.

Thus, through baptism we are incorporated into the body of Christ, His church, and are guaranteed today a future inheritance that will be ours, in actuality, *tomorrow*.

---

1. Alfred Barry, "The Epistle to the Ephesians," in *Ellicott's Commentary on the Whole Bible*, edited by Charles John Ellicott (Grand Rapids, Mich.: Zondervan Publishing House, 1970), p. 20.
2. Joseph A. Grassi, "The Letter to the Ephesians," in *The Jerome*

Biblical Commentary, edited by Raymond E. Brown, Joseph A. Fitzmyer, and Roland E. Murphy (Englewood Cliffs, N.J.: Prentice-Hall, Inc., 1968), p. 344.

3. Henry Chadwick, "Ephesians," *Peake's Commentary on the Bible, edited by Matthew Black and H. H. Rowley (London: Thomas Nelson and Sons, Ltd., 1962), p. 983.*

4. Grassi, p. 344.

5. Chadwick, p. 983.

CHAPTER
Six

The Importance of Prayer

I do not cease to give thanks for you, remembering you in my prayers" (Ephesians 1:16).

Paul was a praying man. He knew by experience the need for staying in close contact with the Divine. Even before he had accepted Christ as a personal Saviour, while he was still a Pharisee, he had an established routine, praying three times a day. But that is just what prayer was to him then: a routine with an impersonal God. When he encountered Jesus on the road to Damascus, however, prayer ceased being a pious routine and became a personal relationship.

What is prayer? The best definitions of prayer are not really definitions at all, but descriptions couched in metaphorical language. "Prayer is the very sword of the Saints." "Prayer is the highest use to which speech can be put. It is the highest meaning that can be put into words." "Prayer is the heart of religion." "Prayer is intercourse with an Ideal Companion." "Prayer is the opening of the heart to God as to a friend." "Prayer is the key in the hand of faith to unlock heaven's storehouse."[1] My favorite one is another definition by Ellen White: "Prayer is the breath of the soul."[2] Prayer is like a breath of fresh air in a hot, stuffy, suffocating room. Without that breath, we wither and die; but with it, we are revitalized.

65

Life cannot be sustained with any degree of quality without food, air, and exercise. Of these three, air is the most essential. We can last many days without food, many months without exercise, but only a few minutes without air. The same is true of our spiritual life: Bible study is our spiritual food, prayer is our spiritual breath, and witnessing is our spiritual exercise. Of the three, the most essential for sustained spiritual life is prayer—the breath of the soul.

The importance of prayer

How often do we pray? How important is prayer in our life? It all depends on how we view God. George A. Buttrick, in his important study on prayer, declares:

> If God is not, "and the life of man, solitary, poore, nasty, brutish, and short," prayer is the veriest self-deceit. If God is, yet is known only in vague rumor and dark coercion, prayer is whimpering folly: it were nobler to die. But if God is in some deep and eternal sense like Jesus, friendship with Him is our first concern, worthiest art, best resource, and sublimest joy. Such prayer could brood over our modern disorder, as the Spirit once brooded over the void, to summon a new world.[3]

George Buttrick suggests that three options are open to us with prayer, and all are related to our understanding of God. First, if God does not exist, then prayer is self-deceit. We are just talking to ourselves. The second option is equally bad: If God exists but is distant, inaccessible, and unknown, then prayer is an impossible task, and we die spiritually.

However, if God in any way resembles Jesus of Nazareth, then "friendship with Him is our first concern, worthiest art, best resource, and sublimest joy." With such a God, prayer becomes the means of summoning a new world order.

The apostle Paul held such a concept of God. Prior to his Damascus road experience, his grasp of God was like the second option—distant, inaccessible, and unknown. With such an understanding of God, prayer was remote, routine, and by rote. Or, as the prophet Isaiah describes it, "This people draw near

66

with their mouth and honor me with their lips, while their hearts are far from me, and their fear of me is a commandment of men learned by rote" (Isaiah 29:13). Because God was exclusive, Paul was also exclusive, intolerant, and a spiritual and social bigot. He was a "Hebrew born of Hebrews" (Philippians 3:5), meaning, among other things, that he was a "racist of racists," persecuting anyone who aspired to a different faith.

When Saul encountered Jesus of Nazareth as Lord and Saviour, his attitude toward others changed because his understanding of God was now different. God was not remote. Rather, He was like Jesus, who took on human form and became one with us—intimate and incarnate. The persecutor of the church and the hater of Gentiles now became the church's greatest spokesman and the lightbearer to the Gentiles. Prayer became the bridge over troubled waters, the sustainer of life between heaven and earth, that which gave him hope even in the midst of the most hopeless situation—imprisonment.

Paul's prayer purpose in Ephesians

When Paul reflects on the experience of the Ephesian Christians, he praises God for their faith: "For this reason, because I have heard of your faith in the Lord Jesus and your love toward all the saints" (chap. 1:15). Faith in the Lord Jesus results in love toward all the saints—*all* the saints. Faith and love go together—faith in God *and* love toward one another. That is the combination. The Laodicean church lacks this faith and love. Jesus counsels them to buy it in the form of *gold* (see Revelation 3:18).

Notice who sells this gold: Jesus—"The Amen, the faithful and true witness, the beginning of God's creation" (Revelation 3:14). God is seeking to return humanity to the relationship they had with Him and with each other in the beginning. God is therefore creating a new humanity in the church—a humanity rich in gold, which is faith in God, manifested in genuine love toward one another.

Above all else, the Laodicean church members need this gold of heaven—the unity of faith and love—in their inter-human relations. Yet all too often we have instead the dross of earth, the cosmetic façade of racial unity, more like a Hollywood prop, behind which is a barren waste. Such a cosmetic façade leads its holders to think themselves rich, prosperous, and in need of nothing, when all along they need gold refined by the fire of God's Spirit, removing the prejudices and cultural blemishes that prevent unity in the church.

Paul sees that the Ephesians have this gold from the divine Goldsmith. Thus he declares, "For this reason, because I have heard of your faith in the Lord Jesus and your love toward all the saints, I do not cease to give thanks for you, remembering you in my prayers" (chap. 1:15, 16).

The main thought of this passage is Paul's concern that the Ephesians may receive a full spiritual understanding of the mystery of God's plan to unite Jew and Gentile as one new humanity in Christ. This is the principal concern of his prayer and the reason why he does not cease praying for them (see verses 17-23).

Notice the spiritual riches in some of the phrases in verses 17-23. "That God . . . may give you a spirit of wisdom and of revelation in the knowledge of him" (verse 17). Joseph Grassi declares that "this knowledge is not a conceptual knowledge of facts as emphasized by the Greeks,"[4] which dominates Western thinking. Paul uses the word *knowledge* in the Semitic sense: "A knowledge that comes from the experience of a person, rather than an acquired conceptual knowledge in the Greek sense."[5]

In Ephesians the Greek word *epignosis* "denotes not knowledge merely of God's plan, but knowledge 'of him,' an experience of God's great love for [humankind] in Christ that would be visibly shown in a true [sister/brotherhood of people] who had previously been divided by so many social and racial barriers."[6]

"The immeasurable greatness of his power in us who believe" (verse 19). This phrase, which describes the power of God, is found nowhere else in the New Testament except here and in Ephesians 3:7. "It expresses the theme of God's mighty power overcoming humanly impossible obstacles."[7] God's plan is to make of the church a visible new humanity, where people are no longer divided by the racial, social, and sexual barriers that dominate relationships in the world at the personal, national, and international levels. From a human perspective this seems impossible. But Paul tells us that the "immeasurable greatness of God's power" is able to accomplish this in us who believe!

It is vital to understand that this unity in diversity in Christ, which results in a new humanity wherein there is neither Jew nor Greek, slave nor free, male nor female, is being worked out by God *in the church*, and not in the world. " 'In the world you have tribulation,' " Jesus said, " 'but be of good cheer, I have overcome the world' " (John 16:33). In light of what we see happening in the world today, what does Jesus mean by "I have overcome the world"? In what way has He "overcome" the world, since there is no peace in the world and racism is rampant?

Jesus does not mean that He has brought peace to the world, for reality speaks otherwise. Rather, He means that He has overcome *the world in the life of the Christian* so that *in the church* there is peace; the world no longer operates in the church and is therefore unable to overcome it. It is *in the church* that God is seeking to manifest His new humanity, not in the world. The world, in turn, will see this new humanity, united in Christ, and it will praise God, and many will acknowledge Him as Lord (see John 17:23).

Can you imagine the grand laughs Satan must have over the news of "Christians" fighting against the Druze in the Middle East; of "Christian" Protestants fighting against "Christian" Catholics in Ireland; of "Christian" White Afrikaners dehumanizing "Christian" Black Africans in South Africa; and of White and Black "Christians" in America praying to the same God but hating each other?

The task of bringing unity in diversity seems humanly impossible. But in this text Paul tells us that God's mighty power *will* overcome humanly impossible obstacles. Thus, in Ephesians 1:21, Paul says that Christ's rule is above "all rule and authority and power and dominion, and above every name that is named, not only in this age but also in that which is to come." Christ has conquered all forms of power so that it can have no hold over His people. Nothing will stand in the way of God's plan for humankind in Christ, for the immeasurable greatness of His power will operate in us who believe. Notice the key phrase, "In us *who believe*." It is not those who say, "Lord, Lord," who shall enter the kingdom of heaven, but "he who does the will of my Father who is in heaven. On that day many will say to me, 'Lord, Lord, did we not prophesy in your name, and cast out demons in your name, and do many mighty works in your name?' [If the Laodicean church is known for anything, it is known for its many "works."] And then will I declare to them, 'I never knew you; depart from me, you evildoers' " (Matthew 7:21-23).

One passage in Ephesians closes by saying that God "has put all things under his [Christ's] feet and has made him the head over all things for the church" (verse 22). This expression goes back to the Garden of Eden, when God told Adam to subdue the earth and have dominion over it (see Genesis 1:28). The old Adam failed, and since that time the world has held dominion over the human race. Christ, the new Adam, the Head of a new humankind, has conquered where the old Adam failed. He has brought to virtual completion Adam's assignment from God to dominate the world, for Paul declares that this domination of the world will be visible in the church. God has made Christ "the head over all things *for the church*, which is his body, the fullness of him who fills all in all" (verses 22, 23, emphasis supplied).

Right here, at the beginning of this most precious letter to the Christian church, Paul prays that the Ephesians will understand what God is seeking to do in the church. He prays this prayer because such understanding is beyond human capability, especially in view of all the bombarding stimuli from the world that influences us to think and behave otherwise.

Conclusion
Can we now understand the importance of prayer in the life of the Christian? Without it there can be no racial and sexual unity in the church. Its importance, however, resides in our

concept of God. That is why a proper concept of God is the key to everything the Christian does or does not do. Paul prayed that the Ephesians would have this understanding of God, which has been revealed by Christ and which results in a new humanity, the visible manifestation of which is the church.

This is the kind of praying we must do. Peter Taylor Forsyth, the great English preacher, declares, "To begin the day with prayer is but a formality unless it goes on in prayer, unless for the rest of it we pray in deed what we began in word."[8]

That is praying! And it is the kind of praying the church must be about!

1. Francis Thompson, "Health and Holiness," cited by George A. Buttrick, *Prayer* (New York: Pilar Books, 1977), p. 16; P. T. Forsyth, *The Soul of Prayer* (Grand Rapids, Mich.: Wm. B. Eerdmans, 1916), p. 18; George A. Buttrick, *Prayer* (New York: Pilar Books, 1977), p. 16; William James, *Psychology: Briefer Course* (New York: Henry Holt and Co., 1892), p. 192, cited by Buttrick; Ellen G. White, *Steps to Christ* (Washington, D.C.: Review and Herald, 1908), pp. 93, 94.

2. Ellen G. White, *Gospel Workers* (Washington, D.C.: Review and Herald, 1915), p. 254.

3. Buttrick, p. 15.

4. Joseph A. Grassi, "The Letter to the Ephesians," in *The Jerome Biblical Commentary*, edited by Raymond E. Brown, Joseph A. Fitzmyer, and Roland E. Murphy (Englewood Cliffs, N.J.: Prentice-Hall, Inc., 1968), p. 343.

5. *Ibid.*, p. 336.

6. *Ibid.*, p. 344.

7. *Ibid.*, p. 346.

8. Forsyth, p. 28.

CHAPTER
Seven

Doing What Comes Naturally

"I n the past you were spiritually dead because of your disobedience and sins. At that time you followed the world's evil way; you obeyed the ruler of the spiritual powers in space, the spirit who now controls the people who disobey God. Actually all of us were like them and lived according to our natural desires, doing whatever suited the wishes of our own bodies and minds. . . . We, like everyone else, were destined to suffer God's anger" (Ephesians 2:1-3, TEV).

Doing what comes naturally. That has been the cry of every generation of pleasure seekers since Eve decided to do "the natural thing," for no matter how one visualizes it, "the natural thing" is always "my own thing." And no matter how much we may think it is our own thing, it turns out to be Satan's. Eve was only doing what Satan wanted her to do. And that is the point Paul makes here at the beginning of chapter 2: "In which you once walked, . . . following the prince of the power of the air" (verse 2). What we think is our own thing turns out to be Satan's. That is the practice of every person before he or she begins to live by the principles of Christ.

The nature of saving grace

Paul's point is this: What we think is the natural thing is really the wrong thing. Doing the natural thing means living contrary to God's plan when He created us at the beginning. For doing what comes naturally means a life of disobedience, sin, and evil desires and actions. That was not God's purpose in creating us. Prior to sin, doing what came naturally meant doing the will and pleasure of God and living by His principles. But, as a result of giving our allegiance to another master, we experienced death—spiritual death that alters the meaning of doing the natural thing. The natural thing (God's way) has now become unnatural, and the unnatural thing (Satan's way) has become natural. But all of this has now been reversed by God's abundant mercy toward us:

> God's mercy is so abundant, and his love for us is so great, that while we were spiritually dead in our disobedience he brought us to life with Christ. It is by God's grace that you have been saved. In our union with Christ Jesus he raised us up with him to rule with him in the heavenly world. He did this to demonstrate for all time to come the extraordinary greatness of his grace in the love he showed us in Christ Jesus. For it is by God's grace that you have been saved through faith. It is not the result of your own efforts, but God's gift, so that no one can boast about it. God has made us what we are, and in our union with Christ Jesus he has created us for a life of good deeds, which he has already prepared for us to do (verses 4-10, TEV).

Now, through grace, the natural thing (the world's evil way) has become unnatural, and the previously unnatural thing (Christ's way) has become natural. That is grace! That is also conversion—a complete turnaround! This is what Ellen White means when she writes:

> All true obedience comes from the heart. It was heart work with Christ. And if we consent, He will so identify Himself with our thoughts and aims, so blend our hearts and minds into conformity to His will, that when obeying Him we shall be but carrying out our own impulses.[1]

73

Doing what comes naturally. How is this divine change possible? Through Jesus Christ, the most "unnatural," yet "natural" person who ever walked this earth.

Ephesians 2:1-10 begins with both Gentile and Jew doing the natural, evil thing. But the passage ends at verse 10 with both still doing the natural thing—the good deeds for which God has prepared us. But these "natural" things are opposite. What makes the difference? The grace of God!

In between the two "natural" behaviors, which are unnatural to each other, we find three amazing acts of God, that, upon closer inspection, are really three phases of one supernatural act (see verses 5, 6):

1. Brought to life with Christ.
2. Raised with Christ.
3. Rule with Christ.

These three expressions are another way of speaking about justification, sanctification, and glorification. Justification means being brought to life with Christ from an experience of death; sanctification means being raised up with Christ in a daily experience of renewal and growth; and glorification means being enthroned with Christ in glory, in the heavenly world. All three expressions have one common denominator: "With Christ." None of this is natural to the sinful human condition. It is all of God, or as Paul declares in verse 9, "It is not the result of your own efforts, but God's gift, so that no one can boast about it" (TEV).

That's grace—reclaiming, redeeming, restoring grace!

As a result of this grace, our behavior changes. Jew now loves Gentile. The Christian no longer behaves like the people who disobey God, for a different spirit is operating within— the spirit of Christ instead of the spirit of Satan.

With the basic theme of this letter in mind (that through Christ the social and racial barriers dividing the human family are removed, resulting in one new humanity in Christ), neither individual Christians nor the institutions they construct can continue behaving the same way as those who are controlled by the ruler of spiritual darkness. This latter mode of living is the way of spiritual death, disobedience, and sin. Christians and their institutions, if they truly deserve the name, must reflect that triple union with Christ—brought to life together with Him, raised together with Him, and enthroned together with Him.

All of this is by way of introduction for what Paul will say in verses 11 to 22: that Christ has broken down the dividing wall of hostility, symbolic of a whole system of racial segregation, and has made one new humanity in Christ out of two that were estranged. But that is the subject matter of our next chapter.

Here, Paul wants us to understand and experience grace— total and complete, fully self-sufficient, wholly undeserved, God's overflowing love for us. Only this grace is able to change a person who is dead in trespasses and sins—doing the evil that comes naturally—and change him or her into something unnatural.

That is grace—saving grace!

"God's mercy is so abundant, and his love for us is so great, that while we were spiritually dead in our disobedience he brought us to life with Christ. It is by God's grace that you have been saved" (verse 4, TEV).

Experiencing this grace

Have you experienced this saving grace? Have you been saved from the world's evil ways?

Most people may say, "Why, of course, I was converted many years ago when I accepted the Lord as my personal Saviour and was baptized. I know that I am saved, and I have personal assurance of my standing with God." This basic Christian theological truth with its emphasis on righteousness by faith has led many a person, who before had no assurance of salvation, to now have that assurance. "The work of righteousness shall be peace; and the effect of righteousness quietness and assurance for ever" (Isaiah 32:17, KJV). Praise the Lord for that!

But that is not what Paul is talking about in Ephesians. The salvation by grace that he speaks of in chapter 2:8—"by grace you have been saved through faith"—cannot be divorced from its context, the hostility between Jew and Gentile. In Ephesians salvation by grace means more than a personal relationship with God. It includes a *social* relationship with our fellow human beings, especially that human being whom the world has taught us to despise as inferior, and, therefore, as less human than ourselves, whether the person be White, Black, Brown, or Yellow. We all suffer from prejudice and acts of pride and superiority. To be saved by grace in Ephesians means to be *saved from these attitudes of prejudice and acts of prideful superiority by the all-powerful grace of God.*

Some may say, "But, I *am* converted!" Keep in mind that historically, beginning with "Saint Peter," the greatest acts of racial bigotry and injustice, sexual discrimination, and prejudice, have been committed, and are even now *being* committed, by so-called "converted Christians."

Conversion means to "turn around," "to return," "to go in the opposite direction one was going" (see Isaiah 44:21, 22; 55: 6, 7; Jeremiah 24:7; Hosea 14:1, 2; Malachi 3:7; Acts 3:19; 1 Peter 2:25). Conversion is a turning back to God from a life of sin, with a contrite and humble heart (see Isaiah 57:15). This turning to God may be so intense that it shakes one emotionally and brings tears, as in Peter's case. However, it can also be a quiet, intellectual acceptance, as with Nicodemus. Or, as with Paul, it can be a dramatic event. No one experience is normative for everyone. God takes into consideration that each of us is different and that our psychological makeups and cultural experiences vary from individual to individual. God meets us where we are, and all He asks is that we respond to Him the best way we know how.

We need to understand conversion in all its dimensions. Recall Peter's conversion experience in Gethsemane, after denying Christ three times. Peter bitterly confessed his wrong and was converted, as Jesus had promised (see Luke 22:32). The result was Pentecost, where thousands responded to Peter's preaching and confessed Christ as Saviour and Lord. However, Peter's conversion did not totally remove his prejudice toward Gentiles, so God gave him a special revelation in the form of a vision about clean and unclean animals, thereby showing him that "God shows no partiality" (Acts 10:34). In other words, God is not a racist! Yet even with this new understanding of God and this new experience of racial integration, Peter slipped back into his old ways at Antioch.

We need to be converted *every single day*. Every day we must be saved by grace, for the social forces of bigotry, prejudice, and racism around us are daily conscripting us into their service. Or, as the Phillips version declares, we are "[drifting] along on the stream of this world's ideas of living" (Ephesians 2:1). This is why Karl Mannheim, the noted German sociologist, declares:

> To live consistently, in the light of Christian brotherly love, in a society which is not organized on the same principle is impossible. The individual in his personal conduct is always compelled—in so far as he does not resort to breaking up the existing social structure—to fall short of his own nobler motives.[2]

Though humanly impossible, this *is* possible by God's grace, for Jesus Christ, through His life and ministry, broke up the existing social structure and tore down the dividing wall of hostility, the social barrier of race, class, and gender (see Ephesians 2:11, 22). This act enables those who have placed their complete trust in Him to live by the new divine ethic of love that enables the Christian to begin doing *naturally* (loving others) that which the world regards as *unnatural*.

---

1. Ellen G. White, *The Desire of Ages* (Mountain View, Calif.: Pacific Press, 1898), p. 668.
2. Karl Mannheim, *Ideology and Utopia* (New York: Harvest Books, 1936), p. 195.

Eight

No Longer Strangers

February is Black history month throughout the United States. Most academic institutions celebrate aspects of Black history in one form or another. The same can be said of African-American congregations. However, I dare say that most Caucasian, Hispanic, and Asian congregations have not even heard of Black history month. Adventist colleges, along with other academic institutions, celebrate America's Black heritage because African-American students in these institutions have pressured their administrations to recognize the immense contribution that African-Americans have made to the development of the United States. So also have the Chinese, Hispanics, Native Americans, and other oppressed groups that have not been given the historical recognition and social value they deserve.

My point is that unless a group puts forth conscious, deliberate effort to be sensitive to the needs of others, these others will go largely unnoticed, unrecognized, and unappreciated. They will remain strangers and aliens, separated and segregated from the rest, often helpless and without hope in the world.

The Gentile condition

Such was the condition of the Gentiles in the midst of Jewish Christianity in the first century:

> Remember that at one time you Gentiles in the flesh, called the uncircumcision by what is called the circumcision, which is made in the flesh by hands—remember that you were at that time separated from Christ, alienated from the commonwealth of Israel, and strangers to the covenants of promise, having no hope and without God in the world (Ephesians 2:11, 12).

Who were these Gentiles? The word *gentile* in the New Testament comes from the Greek word *ethne* that means "nation," from which we get the term *ethnic*. From a Jewish perspective the first-century world was divided into Jews and Gentiles. Since the majority of biblical writers were Jews, the Bible also reflects that perspective—Jewish versus non-Jewish. These Gentiles were separated by race, origin, and election from the Jews, the people of God.

One of the signs of being a Jew was circumcision, the external sign of the covenant between Israel and God. Non-Jews were called the "uncircumcised"—a term full of derision. In spite of their conquered state, the Jews were proud of their Jewish heritage, which gave them a nationalistic sense of peoplehood. Such tends to be the case with all minorities, who in their powerlessness seek to maintain a sense of identity. Though outwardly deprived of prestige and power, inwardly they regard themselves as better and so make prominent those features of their subculture that not only make them distinct from others but, in their own eyes, better.

Christians do the same. Since they all believe in Christ as Saviour and adhere to Scripture as God's Word, what's the difference between a Baptist, a Pentecostal, a Catholic, and an Adventist? None, to speak of. They are all Christians! Then why the difference? To show a distinction between themselves and others who may believe the same, each group emphasizes those aspects of the Christian faith that it feels the others have neglected. Thus Baptists focus on baptism by immersion,

Pentecostals on speaking in tongues, Catholics on the centrality of the church, Methodists on God's method of salvation, Lutherans on righteousness by faith, and Adventists on the Sabbath. These teachings are then made "tests of fellowship" for adherence to the group, in order to show a distinction between itself and the rest of Christendom. Each group, by emphasizing its differences, regards itself as the true follower of Christ.

Such was the case with the Israelites. To maintain the distinction between themselves and Gentiles, they not only made the law uppermost, but also strictly enforced a number of other rules and ordinances that legitimized their racial and religious discrimination against others. All of these discriminating rules and regulations, including the moral law itself, served as a "hedge" to segregate Israel from all non-Israelites. They served as "instruments of racial exclusiveness."[1] A first-century document declares: "Our Lawgiver . . . fenced us round with impregnable ramparts and walls of iron that we might not mingle at all with any of the other nations, but remain pure in body and soul."[2] Thus the law, along with many other rules and regulations established to benefit one group at the expense of others, became a means by which racism and ethnic division was propagated. It is very difficult for Christians, for whom the moral law of God—the Ten Commandments—is of utmost importance, to realize that this law had been turned by the Jews into an instrument for the legitimization of institutional racism. But such was the case. The law, which had been given by God as a means to develop moral character in His people, was converted, through the many ordinances derived from its interpretation, into a whole system of negative behaviors and beliefs toward those who did not observe the law. These multiple rules and regulations prestructured choices, so that merely by observing them, individuals consciously or unconsciously practiced discrimination and racism against others.

The hard facts of the matter were given a substantive reality in the construction of a dividing stone wall some four and a half feet high, separating the outer court of the temple from the inner court. In fact, the entire layout excluded non-Jews from entry into the temple, thereby protecting the vested interests of the religious leaders—interests of power and control.

There was the Court of the Gentiles, beyond which foreigners could not go; there was the Court of women, beyond which Jewish women could not pass; then there was the Court of Israel, the men's Court, beyond which Jewish laymen could not enter; and finally there was the Court of priests, where only priests were allowed (see the diagram below):

Solomon's Temple

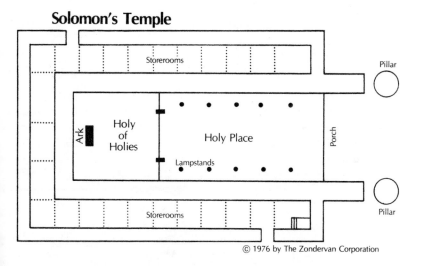

© 1976 by The Zondervan Corporation

None of these courts were part of the original blueprint that God gave to Moses for the construction of the tabernacle in the wilderness (see Exodus 25-27 and 36-40). Neither were they part of Solomon's temple nor of the temple rebuilt after the exile under the ministry of Haggai and Zechariah (see the diagram on the next page):

81

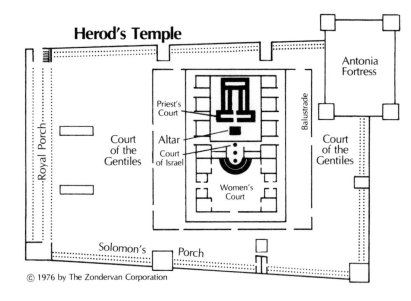

© 1976 by The Zondervan Corporation

The restructuring came later, when Herod the Great rebuilt the temple shortly before the time of Christ. The whole structure then came to serve as a social barrier, giving people little access to God.

Josephus, the first-century Jewish historian, tells us that on this stone wall were inscriptions prohibiting any foreigner from going further, under penalty of death. These inscriptions were written in Greek and Latin, the two languages of the Gentiles: "No stranger [non-Jew] is to enter within the balustrade and enclosure around the Temple. Whoever is caught will be responsible to himself for his death, which will ensue." Like the Berlin Wall, this wall had both a physical and a psychological meaning. And like the Jim Crow laws in the pre-fifties South, and like Apartheid in present-day South Africa, "the stone wall was but a token of a whole system of separation that went into every phase of life."[3]

We cannot begin to understand the feelings of these Palestinian Jews toward Gentiles, Samaritans, and Jews of mixed racial heritage (such as Galileans) unless we under-

82

stand the Jewish insistence on ancestral and racial purity. The Jews held that only Israelites of pure ancestry made up the pure Israel. Thus, "even the simple Israelite knew his immediate ancestors and could point to which of the twelve tribes he belonged."[4]

The books of Ezra, Nehemiah, and 1 and 2 Chronicles, written after the exile, are filled with genealogical lists. Have you ever wondered, in reading through the Bible, why all the fuss over genealogies? After the Assyrian exile, genealogies became especially important in order to separate pure families from those racially mixed as a result of the racial mixing practices of the Assyrians. A person could not be a priest unless he could prove his ancestral purity for at least five generations. No person could hold a public office who was not of pure ancestry, nor would public officials associate in court or in public office with persons whose ancestry was of doubt. Proof of pure ancestry was important in order for a woman to marry into a priestly family.

The most important reason for proof of ancestral purity, however, had to do with religion and salvation. If one came up short of merits in the judgment, the merits of Abraham could be added to one's account and thus assure him of salvation. However, only those who could trace their lineage to Abraham had access to his merits. Thus, a person's salvation depended on his or her ancestral purity. Then, too, prophecy declared that before the end of the age the prophet Elijah would return to "turn the hearts of fathers to their children, and the hearts of children to their fathers" (Malachi 4:6). In other words, Elijah would restore the family to its ancestral purity so that people would be ready for the final salvation.

Joachim Jeremias, the renowned New Testament scholar, declares:

> Only families of pure Israelite descent could be assured of a share in the messianic salvation, for only they were assisted by the "merits of their legitimate ancestry." Here we have the most profound reason for the behavior of these pure Israelite families—why they watched so carefully over the maintenance

of racial purity and examined the genealogies of their future sons- and daughters-in-law before marriage. For on this question of racial purity hung not only the social position of their descendants, but indeed their final assurance of salvation, their share in the future redemption of Israel.[5]

This meant that Gentiles, as well as Jews of mixed heritage, were prevented from holding any position of social merit within the Jewish community because of their racial and cultural mixture. Worse still, they had no share in the final salvation of Israel, but were thought to be despised and rejected, even by God! "Remember that you were at that time separated from Christ, alienated from the commonwealth of Israel, and strangers to the covenants of promise, having no hope and without God in the world" (Ephesians 2:12).

Such was the relationship of Gentiles and Jews in Christ's day. The situation was similar to South Africa today. Like Black South Africans, the Gentiles were segregated, alienated, and strangers, without hope and helpless.

Then Jesus came

Then Jesus came! And all was changed.

> Now in Christ Jesus you who once were far off have been brought near in the blood of Christ. For he is our peace, who has made us both one, and has broken down the dividing wall of hostility, by abolishing in his flesh the law of commandments and ordinances, that he might create in himself one new [person] in place of the two, so making peace, and might reconcile us both to God in one body through the cross, thereby bringing the hostility to an end (Ephesians 2:13-16).

This text declares that Jesus broke down "the dividing wall of hostility, by abolishing in his flesh the law of commandments and ordinances." This means that the Jewish wall of separation and segregation in the temple was undergirded by a whole system of laws, rules, and regulations—the Bible calls them "commandments and ordinances." These laws legitimized Jewish exclusiveness and gave the dividing wall a moral and theological significance. Jesus broke down this dividing wall by show-ing through His life of ministry, His cleansing of the temple, and finally His death on the Cross, that all of these petty re-ligious and social discriminations were incompatible with His mission and the gospel. He thereby removed the very basis for the existence of such divisions. Since God's moral law was used as the basis for these others rules and regulations, in doing away with the latter, Jesus freed the former (the Ten Com-mandments) from its role as an instrument of racial exclusive-ness. He restored the moral law to its proper role as the means by which character is developed.

After cleansing the temple, Jesus declared, " 'My house shall be called a house of prayer for all the nations,' " (Mark 11:17). By this He announced God's new universalism and put an end to all exclusivisms. Henceforth, no one would be ex-cluded from God's presence[6] because of race, class, or gender. In this declaration of universalism, Jesus proclaimed a new redemptive social order: All of God's children are one and have equal access to God. "There is neither Jew nor Greek [no divi-sion based on racial and ethnic differences], there is neither slave nor free [no division based on status and social class], there is neither male nor female [no division based on gender]; for you are all one in Christ Jesus" (Galatians 3:28). This sug-gests that keeping women and ethnic minorities from full access to the temple was a human construction that went con-trary to the purposes of God for all humankind.

Minority and oppressed males are very quick to pick up on racial and class discrimination but rather slow to do the same with discrimination based on gender. And the reason is simple: they themselves oppress. But Christ and the gospel demand the destruction of *all* "dividing walls of hostility" that oppress and discriminate against people.

In identifying with oppressed, multiracial humanity, Jesus put into effect "the Galilean principle: What human beings re-ject, God chooses as his very own."[7] The apostle Paul pro-claims this principle in 1 Corinthians:

Consider your call, brethren; not many of you were wise according to worldly standards, not many were powerful, not many were of noble birth; but God chose what is foolish in the world to shame the wise, God chose what is weak in the world to shame the strong, God chose what is low and despised in the world, even things that are not, to bring to nothing things that are, so that no human being might boast in the presence of God (1:26-29).

That, my friends, is the gospel! When Jesus comes, groups that had been hostile are reconciled.

How would the church be different if Jesus were here today? What would He do differently from what we do that would alter the actions and attitudes of our church? The greatest need of the church today is Jesus—Jesus the Galilean.[8] He is the Christ who identifies with the specific needs of His people, especially the neo-Galileans—the despised, the rejected and neglected, the powerless minorities in our society, the two-thirds majority of the world's population living in the Third World, as well as Third World groups in the First World. For Jesus the Galilean reveals God as the One who has identified with our situation of alienation and dehumanization. He teaches us to reject everything that would belittle and demean us, because our racial and cultural differences do not make us inferior, but special, in the eyes of God.

The new humanity in Christ

This portion of Scripture, including chapter 2:11-22, is the heart of Paul's message to the Ephesians. Everything he has said up to now has this racial reconciliation in mind. The previous section on salvation through grace (verses 1-10) was an introduction to what he declares here. As brought out in the last chapter, salvation by grace includes more than a personal relationship with God. It also includes a social relationship with other human beings, especially those who differ from us in color, class, or culture. Whether we are White, Black, Brown, or Yellow, we all need God's saving grace in this area of interhuman relations.

This is the heart of the message to the Ephesians. "He is

our peace, who has made us both one, and has broken down the dividing wall of hostility, by abolishing in his flesh the law of commandments and ordinances, that he might create in himself one new [person] in place of the two, so making peace" (verses 14, 15). Here is where we get the concept of "the new humanity in Christ." "It is not merely a question of the Gentiles joining the Jews; a new basis of unity and harmony is created in Christ." Those in Christ are a "third race,"[9] if you please. It is now neither Jew nor Gentile, but a new humanity in Christ, the true meeting place of the nations, the "Geneva" of racial and religious politics.

Jesus is not going to save Greeks and Jews, or Blacks and Whites, or Hispanics and Asians, or Italians and Germans, or Irish and English, or West Indians and Africans, or Americans and Russians, or Armenians and Azerbaijanis, or Israelis and Palestinians, or Pakistanis and Indians, or Iraquis and Iranians, or Japanese and Chinese. He is going to save a "new humanity" who have risen by God's grace above ethnocentric worldviews, prejudicial attitudes, political ideologies, and racist actions, to become the "new men" and "new women"— the new humanity—in Christ. The people whom Jesus will save are those who exemplify in all their attitudes and actions genuine, compassionate Christian love toward others. They are the ones who, though not denying or belittling their proud ethnic heritage, rise above this heritage to their new identity in Christ as sons and daughters of God and as members of His divine family (see Ephesians 2:20).

But how is this possible? How is Christ able to do it? Verse 17 gives us the answer: "He came and preached peace to you who were far off and peace to those who were near." He preached peace to both parties. This expression comes from Isaiah 57:

And it shall be said,
"Build up, build up, prepare the way,
    remove every obstruction from my people's way."
For thus says the high and lofty One
    who inhabits eternity, whose name is Holy:

87

"I dwell in the high and holy place,
and also with him who is of a contrite and humble spirit,
to revive the spirit of the humble,
and to revive the heart of the contrite.
For I will not contend for ever,
nor will I always be angry;
for from me proceeds the spirit,
and I have made the breath of life.
Because of the iniquity of his covetousness I was angry,
I smote him, I hid my face and was angry;
but he went on backsliding in the way of his own heart.
I have seen his ways, but I will heal him;
I will lead him and requite him with comfort,
creating for his mourners the fruit of the lips.
Peace, peace, to the far and to the near, says the Lord;
and I will heal him.
But the wicked are like the tossing sea;
for it cannot rest,
and its waters toss up mire and dirt.
There is no peace, says my God, for the wicked "
(verses 14-21, emphasis supplied).

It is God's purpose to "remove every obstruction from [His] people's way" (verse 14). But God can bring about healing only where there is a humble spirit. The sin that God abhors above every other sin is pride, for pride knows no need. And the worst form of pride is racial pride, the greatest sin plaguing the church today, which is preventing the gospel from reaching the masses of humanity suffering under all forms of oppression.

In 1890 Union College was established in College View, Nebraska. The school was developed as a multi-language school to serve the needs of Danish, Swedish, Norwegian, German, and English students. Fairly quickly it became primarily a German, Scandinavian, and English school, with separate facilities for each of the three groups, including separate dining rooms, chapels, and classrooms, resulting in "duplicate comforts, conveniences, and necessary appliances."[10]

The motive for such an arrangement seemed worthy enough. At that time in American history, the various

European language groups that had settled in the United States still maintained strong cultural identities. The Adventists among these groups were anxious both to preserve their cultural identity and to evangelize their own people. Thus it seemed to them reasonable to arrange for their children to receive their college education in a culturally exclusive environment.

By the mid-1890s the young people had tired of the artificial arrangement, and the college administration acceded to their request for a unified school. However, their elders back home were not so easily persuaded to give up their biases. By the year 1905 a movement was underway to establish separate English, German, and Scandinavian conference structures in the Central Union. Fortunately, Ellen White recognized the danger and wrote strongly against it, and no such structures were ever established.[11] But Ellen White's advice makes it clear that more was involved than effective evangelism among national groups. Ethnic rivalry was threatening to break up the unity of God's people, particularly among the publishing workers.

With such a situation in mind, Ellen White wrote in 1905 the following words, now famous for their importance, but first written because of ethnic conflict in the church:

> If we would humble ourselves before God, and be kind and courteous and tenderhearted and pitiful, there would be one hundred conversions to the truth where now there is only one. But, though professing to be converted, we carry around with us a bundle of self that we regard as altogether too precious to be given up. [12]

Many are the times that this statement has been quoted in sermons and applied to personal religion and our personal relationship with God, when its original context was social/ethnic conflict in the church. What is this "bundle of self that we regard as altogether too precious to be given up"? It is ethnic pride. And it leads one group to regard itself as better than another group. Pride is the worst sin, for it knows no need.[13]

Keep in mind that this was uttered in view of a problem existing, not between Blacks and Whites, but between various groups of northern European Whites, who for all practical purposes looked alike, but who could not get along because of ethnic pride. The result was a lack of church growth. Ellen White said that if believers would change, there would be "one hundred conversions to the truth where now there is only one." That would have been a phenomenal change in the rate of church growth. Could this have been a factor leading to the rejection of the 1888 message of righteousness by faith by the Seventh-day Adventist Church in the years following the Minneapolis Conference? Keep in mind that Minnesota is the home state of Swedes, Danes, and Germans.

If Ellen White's statement was true then due to the conflict between white Germans and white Danes, and between white Swedes and white Norwegians, imagine the greater application of that statement today in the conflict between Whites, Blacks, and Browns, or between African Americans who cannot get along with West Indians, or Hispanics with other Hispanics, or Asians with other Asians, or Africans with other Africans, or Americans with Soviets, or First World people with Third World people, etc. No wonder we are not experiencing the kind of growth we should! We may talk of evangelism, church growth, and the caring church, but unless we humble ourselves—stop thinking of our own ethnic group as better and more deserving of special financial privileges, leadership privileges, and positional privileges—we will not see the "one hundred conversions to the truth where now there is only one." On the following page Ellen White goes on to declare:

> Christ recognized no distinction of nationality or rank or creed. The scribes and Pharisees desired to make a local and a national benefit of all the gifts of heaven and to exclude the rest of God's family in the world. But Christ came to break down every wall of partition. . . . The life of Christ established a religion in which there is no caste, a religion by which Jew and Gentile, free and bond, are linked in a common brotherhood, equal before God.[14]

No longer strangers

Ephesians 2:18 declares, "Through him we both have access in one Spirit to the Father." The word *access* (Greek *prosagoges*) denoted the person in Oriental courts who introduced others into the presence of the king. Christ became the *prosagoges* who took two separated children, Jew and Gentile, Galilean Jew and Judean Jew, African-American and White American, White South African and Black South African, Mexican and Argentinean, Irish and English, Israeli and Palestinian, Armenian and Azerbaijanis—the list is infinite—and "preached peace" to both, thereby uniting them as brothers, and brought them into the intimacy of God's family as members of God's household. The picture here is reminiscent of the compassionate father in Luke 15 who tries to unite the prodigal son and the elder brother, while the banquet and all the festivities are waiting to be experienced by both in love.[15] The result, for those who allow themselves to be united, is that they are no longer strangers, but fellow citizens and members of the household of God (verses 19-22).

God is a God of unity and love, not of discord and hatred. Where there is union and love, there God will make a dwelling place of peace. Such is God's desire for the church. Yet from the church the cry of the saints goes up, "How long, Lord? How long till this night of weeping turn to a morn of song?" And from heaven comes back the answer, "Till we allow the Prince of peace to create peace in our hearts toward one another, thereby enabling our churches to become a 'house of peace for all nations.' "

---

1. Henry Chadwick, "Ephesians," *Peake's Commentary on the Bible*, edited by Matthew Black and H. H. Rowley (London: Thomas Nelson and Sons, Ltd., 1962), p. 983.

2. "Letter of Aristeas," cited by Chadwick, p. 983.

3. See Josephus, *Antiquities of the Jews*, book XV: xi:5 (Grand Rapids, Mich.: Kregel Publications, 1960), p. 336. Siegfried H. Horn, "Temple," in *Seventh-day Adventist Bible Dictionary* (Washington, D.C.: Review and Herald Publishing Association, 1960), p. 1079.

Joseph A. Grassi, "The Letter to the Ephesians," in *The Jerome Biblical Commentary*, edited by Raymond E. Brown, Joseph A. Fitzmyer, and Roland E. Murphy (Englewood Cliffs, N.J.: Prentice-Hall, Inc., 1968), p. 345.

4. This section on ancestral and racial purity is taken from Joachim Jeremias, *Jerusalem in the Time of Jesus* (Philadelphia, Penn.: Fortress Press, 1969), pp. 275-302.

5. *Ibid.*, pp. 301, 302.

6. See Virgilio Elizondo, *Galilean Journey: The Mexican-American Promise* (Maryknoll, N.Y.: Orbis Books, 1983), p. 73.

7. *Ibid.*, p. 91.

8. See my article, "The Significance of Galilee," Lake Union *Ministerial Digest* 3:2 (Spring 1985), pp. 11-22.

9. Elizondo, p. 73; Chadwick, p. 980.

10. Everett Dick, *Union: College of the Golden Cords* (Lincoln, Neb.: Union College Press, 1967), p. 38. See also "Union College," in *Seventh-day Adventist Encyclopedia*, edited by Don F. Neufeld (Washington, D.C.: Review and Herald, 1966), vol. 10, p. 1515.

11. Ellen G. White, *Testimonies for the Church* (Mountain View, Calif.:, 1948), vol. 9, p. 195.

12. *Ibid.,* p. 189.

13. Ellen G. White, *Steps to Christ* (Mountain View, Calif.: Pacific Press, 1956), p. 30.

14. Ellen G. White, *The Ministry of Healing* (Mountain View, Calif: Pacific Press, 1905), p. 25.

15. For an interesting study of the character of God in Luke 15, see Caleb Rosado, *What Is God Like?* (Hagerstown, Md.: Review and Herald, 1988).

CHAPTER

Nine

The Church: God's Last Hope for Earth

Before we take up the message of Ephesians 3, it might be helpful to go back and review the context and setting of the letter. Verse 1 forces us to do precisely that. "For this reason I, Paul, a prisoner for Christ on behalf of you Gentiles." Paul is in prison—for what reason? Notice that the sentence leaves you hanging. It is an unfinished sentence—a style that is very typical of the apostle Paul. He has so much to say that often his thoughts come out as unfinished sentences. I am sure it was frustrating for the secretary who received his dictation. Sometimes he comes back to a thought and finishes it, but at other times he doesn't. Ephesians 3:1 is a case where he does come back and complete his thought. However, he does not get back to this opening thought until verse 14! The clue, of course, is that he begins the sentence the same way, but this time he completes it:

> For this reason I bow my knees before the Father, from whom every family in heaven and on earth is named, that according to the riches of his glory he may grant you to be strengthened with might through his Spirit in the inner man,

and that Christ may dwell in your hearts through faith; that you, being rooted and grounded in love, may have power to comprehend with all the saints what is the breadth and length and height and depth, and to know the love of Christ which surpasses knowledge, that you may be filled with all the fulness of God (verses 14-19).

This is Paul's complete thought. Again, as in chapter 1:15-23, Paul prays that God will strengthen the Ephesians through the Spirit and give them wisdom to understand the dimensions of Christ's love for them. This section will be discussed in detail in the next chapter.

However, in verse 1, he gets sidetracked and does not complete that thought for thirteen verses. Why the digression? Paul knew that the Ephesians were concerned about his imprisonment—they thought he was in prison on their account. Nothing can discourage a Christian faster than the question of suffering. Why does God allow bad things to happen to good people? How does one speak about God from the suffering of the innocent? The entire book of Job is devoted to this question.[2] Paul's purpose is to give the Ephesians a full understanding of Christ—as he says in chapter 4:13, 14, "Until we all attain to the unity of the faith and of the knowledge of the Son of God, to mature [personhood], to the measure of the stature of the fulness of Christ; so that we may no longer be children." That is Paul's desire. But he is wise enough to realize that people cannot understand such things if they are still tripping on the question of suffering, especially since he is writing from prison. So he digresses from his purposes in order to help his readers understand why Christians have to endure trials and tribulations in this world.

Paul's explanation of suffering

The key point in this section is not so much what Paul says about suffering but *how* he says it. His focus is on how to deal with the problem. Christians so often trip up in their method of handling this most perplexing subject.

Paul does not begin by saying, "This is most unfortunate. I

had some great plans for proclaiming the gospel, but they were interrupted by the inconvenience of imprisonment. Be of good cheer, though. Weeping lasts only for the night; joy comes in the morning. Everything will turn out all right."

Isn't that how we usually do it? We explain why circumstances aren't so bad; how matters could have been much worse. But that is not Paul's method. "What he does . . . is to tell them how he himself looks at it; he shows them his own attitude and reaction to the events. And then he urges them to look at the problem in a like manner."[3] The importance of this method is that it provides us the way by which to face any trial. Here is a proven method that works. So what is it?

First, Paul does not utter a single word of complaint. You hear no sob story here, like: "All these years I have served the Lord. I've been faithful in my stewardship, dedicated to His cause, gotten old in His service, and here I am. Why?" You hear none of this. "Not a word! No complaints, no grumbles!"[4]

Second, there is no stoic, self-resignation to the trials, no stiff upper lip. "In this life we have to take the bad with the good; it's part of life. But keep your chin up; it is darkest just before the dawn. Hang in there; God will see us through." "That is Stoicism, that is paganism, that is the world's so-called courage! It has nothing to do with Christianity; indeed it is almost the very antithesis of it."[5]

A close inspection of this portion of scripture reveals that Paul is not downcast by his experience, but appears to rejoice in the midst of trials! There is a note of triumph, of victory, of glorifying God. Verse 13, at the end of the section, gives a hint of this: "I ask you not to lose heart over what I am suffering for you, which is your glory." Don't get discouraged; we are more than conquerors! Do you recall Paul and Silas's experience in Philippi that is recorded in Acts 16:19, 22-25? They sang and praised God while in stocks in prison. This is not just an isolated incident that only Paul experienced. Peter tells us the same thing in 1 Peter 4:12-14: "Beloved, do not be surprised at the fiery ordeal which comes upon you to prove you, as though something strange were happening to you. But rejoice insofar as you share Christ's sufferings, that you may also rejoice and be glad when his glory is revealed. If you are reproached for the name of Christ, you are blessed, because the spirit of glory and of God rests upon you." James declares the same thing: "Count it all joy, my brethren, when you meet various trials, for you know that the testing of your faith produces steadfastness" (1:2, 3). The point is clear; Paul wants the Ephesians to view his imprisonment and suffering as a means by which God is glorified.

We need to distinguish, however, between trials that we bring on ourselves by our failure to do what is right and trials that are the byproduct of doing right. There is a difference, and Peter brings out that difference in the next two verses: "Let none of you suffer as a murderer, or a thief, or a wrongdoer, or a mischief-maker; yet if one suffers as a Christian, let him not be ashamed, but under that name let him glorify God" (1 Peter 4:15, 16). It is with the latter and not the former experience in mind that Scripture urges us to "count it all joy . . . when you meet various trials" (James 1:2).

How does Paul arrive at this position? This is a most important question for us to consider. The answer is not that Paul has a placid, phlegmatic temperament. He is not a doormat. He is impulsive, aggressive, energetic, yet he can get easily depressed when things do not go his way. Paul's peace of mind is not a matter of temperament but the end product of his method. Dr. Martin Lloyd-Jones describes Paul's method:

> He asks questions, and then, having noted the answers, he works out the argument. This is his invariable method. It is precisely what he does here in this digression. The first thing you and I have to do in this Christian life is to learn that secret. Instead of allowing things to overwhelm us and to depress us, and to make us sit down and commiserate with ourselves, we must stop and look at the circumstances, and ask questions about the thing itself, not about God. Having done so we must note the answers and then work out an argument. We must put the whole matter into its context, into its setting, and relate it to the whole of the Christian faith and life. As we do so we shall find that an argument will emerge.[6]

Why Paul was in prison

Paul is in prison. He knows it, and the Ephesians know it. But why is he there? The first thing he tells us is that he is no ordinary prisoner, but a "prisoner for Christ" (Ephesians 3:1). This isn't a statement of discouragement, but a title of distinction. All of Paul's titles are connected to Christ: "The apostle of Christ," "the servant of Christ," "the minister of Christ," "the slave of Christ." Everything is in terms of being "in Christ"—a favorite Pauline expression of what it means to be a Christian. And now he is "a prisoner of Christ." Not Nero's prisoner or Rome's prisoner or the Jews' prisoner, but Christ's prisoner. What an attitude!

He is not only Christ's prisoner, but a prisoner "on behalf of" the Gentiles, the Ephesians. He is suffering on their account. Why? Verse 1 declares, "For this reason." What reason? For the reason he has just given in the last section of chapter 2: for preaching the message that the saving grace of Jesus Christ has as its basis the removal of ethnic conflict and racial divisions that undermine the very structures and fabric of the church. The apostles and the prophets followed Christ's example, challenging God's people, the institutions of their day, and society to live by principles of justice and mercy in their dealings with one another.

This is the mystery of Christ that Gentiles and Jews who respond to the claims of Christ are united in Christ in spite of their ethnic diversity.

> When you read this you can perceive my insight into the mystery of Christ, which was not made known to the sons of men in other generations as it has now been revealed to his holy apostles and prophets by the Spirit; [and what is this mystery that has now been revealed?] that is, how the Gentiles are fellow heirs, members of the same body, and partakers of the promise in Christ Jesus through the gospel (Ephesians 3:4-6).

Paul is in prison because everywhere he went he preached this "mystery of Christ"—the unity that should exist between Jew and Gentile in Christ. Paul was a preacher not

97

only of personal righteousness, but also and especially of *social righteousness*. His message of righteousness included a strong focus on race and intergroup relations. It was this, more than anything else he did, that infuriated the Jews and caused them to turn against him. A message of personal righteousness seldom gets people angry at the preacher, because the focus is on the "private" side of religion. But a message of social righteousness, focusing on the "public" side of one's faith, will always anger the masses. Examples of this are Jesus' first sermon in Nazareth (see Luke 4:16-30), Gandhi in India, Martin Luther King, Jr. in the streets of America, Desmond Tutu and Allan Boesak in South Africa. When people know they are doing wrong, and when that wrong is based on racial pride and someone tells them about the right way, they will get angry and retaliate. The Jews' hatred of the Gentiles was so great that they, too, erected an entire system of apartheid—segregation—by which to maintain a distinction between themselves and the Gentiles. This was physically and psychologically symbolized by the stone wall in the temple, beyond which no Gentile could go under penalty of death.

The actual account of Paul's arrest and the reason for it are found in Acts 21 and 22,[7] which make it clear that he was arrested for preaching, not just that the Gentiles had equal access to God, but that because of the gospel, the Jews were to treat the Gentiles as brothers and sisters and joint heirs with themselves in Christ. Such truth was intolerable to the Jews, and they wanted him killed.

Had Paul stuck to a message of personal salvation and the saving grace of Christ to the individual believer, he might have been all right. No criticism, no incarceration, no chopping block. The famed English preacher Dr. Martin Lloyd-Jones says, "Some of us would be much more popular in the Church, as well as in the world, if we did not say certain things. If a preacher wants to be popular he must never offend."[8] But Paul was not out to win a popularity contest, but to do the will of God. "The love of Christ constrains us," he declared (2 Corinthians 5:14, NKJV). If only he had withheld this particular aspect of his message, everything would have been fine. But it wasn't *his* message, and therefore not his prerogative what to include and what to leave out. "I was told to preach it," he declares in Ephesians 3:7-9:

> Of this gospel I was made a minister according to the gift of God's grace which was given me by the working of his power. To me, though I am the very least of all the saints, this grace was given, to preach to the Gentiles the unsearchable riches of Christ, and to make all men see what is the plan of the mystery hidden for ages in God who created all things.

Thus Paul begins chapter 3 by telling the Ephesians, "For this reason I, Paul, a prisoner for Christ Jesus on behalf of you Gentiles" (verse 1). "I am in prison because of you," he says. "I am in prison so that you might enjoy the liberty of the gospel. Had I withheld that portion of the message, I would still be free, but you wouldn't. You would still be in prison—the prison of [separation] from Christ, [alienation] from the commonwealth of Israel, and [being] 'strangers to the covenants of promise, having no hope and without God in the world'" (chap. 2:12). There is no worse prison than being shut out from God's presence. Satan himself will experience this prison during the millennium (see Revelation 20).

This is why Paul is suffering. He wants the Ephesians to understand the purpose behind suffering and Christ's suffering on their behalf. Many of these Ephesians were slaves who had very little in this world. The gospel gave them a new lease on life, a purpose for existence, a new identity. They were no longer slaves, no longer Gentiles, no longer women (all positions of low prestige and social worth in the eyes of the Jews), but sons and daughters of God! Christ died for them, showing what their true value was. And Paul now lets them know that he counts it a privilege to be suffering in prison on their behalf. Such a statement of faith lifted the Ephesians from the doldrums of doubt and despair to the divine dimensions of God's love for them. And it will lift anyone found in similar social and spiritual circumstances.

Paul thus tells Christians of every age how to face suffering and trials: by understanding the meaning behind the event. He therefore declares in Philippians 1:29, "It has been granted to you that for the sake of Christ you should not only believe in him but also suffer for his sake."

God's last hope for earth

But Paul is still not through declaring to the Ephesians the reason why he is preaching such a radical message. Notice verses 10 to 12:

> That through the church the manifold wisdom of God might now be made known to the principalities and powers in the heavenly places. This was according to the eternal purpose which he has realized in Christ Jesus our Lord, in whom we have boldness and confidence of access through our faith in him.

Paul means that God has a plan, hidden for the ages in God, but now revealed. And what is that plan? "That *through the church* the manifold wisdom of God might now be made known to the principalities and powers in the heavenly places." This gospel is to be made manifest in the church—in its present reality!

In other words, before Christ comes back to receive His own, His church—the new humanity in Christ—will reflect in their collective experience, both in worship and structured fellowship, at the personal and institutional levels, this unity in diversity in Christ. And this manifestation of community, which appears to be so humanly impossible in this present age of ethnic, racial, and national conflicts, will be such a living reality in the church that it will amaze even the demonic powers in heavenly places, which have been the force behind all the racial, social, and political conflict in the world and among God's people since the beginning of time.

Ellen White declares that "the church is the repository of the riches of the grace of Christ; and through the church will eventually be made manifest, even to 'the principalities and powers in heavenly places,' the final and full display of the love of God."[9]

Thus the church is God's last hope for planet Earth. The last message to be preached by the church is "the full display of the love of God." And how is that love displayed? John tells us in 1 John 4:20, "If any one says, 'I love God,' and hates his brother, he is a liar; for he who does not love his brother whom he has seen, cannot love God whom he has not seen. And this commandment we have from him, that he who loves God should love his brother also."

Paul declares that this has always been God's eternal purpose for His church (see Ephesians 3:11). Therefore we are not to lose heart over the sufferings we experience due to injustice (verse 13), but must confront those injustices through our practice and preaching. Like Paul, we must not cease preaching this message just because it is unpopular. We must preach it because it is God's purpose for His people, which will in the end bring glory to Him.

That is our purpose for existence as Christians in the world today. And to this mission we must be faithful in all our attitudes and actions.

---

1. Credit for the general outline and theme of this chapter is given to D. Martin Lloyd-Jones's study on Ephesians, *The Unsearchable Riches of Christ: An Exposition of Ephesians 3:1-21* (Grand Rapids, Mich.: Baker Book House, 1979).

2. See the excellent book by Gustavo Gutierrez, which seeks to answer this question: *Hablar de Dios desde el sufrimiento del inocente: Una reflexión sobre el libro de Job* (Lima, Peru: Institutio Barolomé de Las Casas, 1986), published in English as *On Job: God-Talk and the Suffering of the Innocent* (Maryknoll, N.Y.: Orbis Books, 1987).

3. Lloyd-Jones, p. 16.

4. *Ibid.*

5. *Ibid.,* p. 17.

6. *Ibid.,* p. 18.

7. See chapter 2 of this book.

8. Lloyd-Jones, p. 22.

9. Ellen G. White, *The Acts of the Apostles* (Mountain View, Calif.: Pacific Press, 1911), p. 9.

Ten

The Prayer of All Nations

Paul's letter to the Ephesians is the grand climax of his theology. For some thirty years he has preached a gospel of redemption, reconciliation, and righteousness, which affects not only the relationship of humans to God but also their relationship to each other.

As a result of Paul's preaching in first-century Palestine, people were moved by their new reconciliation to God, but disturbed by their new relationship to fellow humans. That has been the case throughout history. "Go ahead, preach your pious sermons!" the masses have told the preachers of every age. "Speak of God and how good He is and how wonderful His love; tell us to love Him and put our trust in Him; but don't tell us that as a consequence of that love we must love our fellow human beings, especially those who differ from us. Now you have stopped preaching and have gone to meddling!"

So thought the Jews of Paul's day, and they had him arrested for preaching a gospel that saved not only them but also the Gentiles. Even more, Paul preached that as a result of the gospel, Jew and Gentile were equal—sons and daughters of God, brothers and sisters in Christ. Heresy! cried the Jews, and they incited a riot, falsely accusing Paul so that the Romans could put him away (see Acts 21 and 22).

Now he found himself in prison, but not wasting away. Rather, he reflected on the reasons why he was there. In chapter 3:1 he begins to pray for the Ephesians, but he immediately digresses to explain why he is suffering for God on their behalf. He concludes the digression in verse 13: "I ask you not to lose heart over what I am suffering for you, which is your glory." Take heart! Rejoice with me, for my imprisonment is the result of preaching God's eternal purpose for His church. This purpose will amaze even the powers and principalities in heavenly places. And what is that purpose? That through the church, God will bring about unity in diversity among all nations within the church—a reality that is impossible in the world.

Paul then begins again what he started thirteen verses earlier: "For this reason . . ." What reason? The reason enunciated in chapter 2: that God has made Jews and Gentiles, who were enemies in the world without hope of reconciliation, one new humanity in Christ, and at peace with each other and with God. He has broken down the divisions of hostility, thereby creating one church where exists oneness in Christ. "For this reason," Paul says, "I bow my knees [in prayer] before the Father" (verse 14). Paul now enters into a prayer that could easily be called "The prayer of all nations." And each phrase of this prayer could easily be elaborated into a separate sermon. In this letter, written near the end of his earthly life, Paul's theology reaches a maturity not found in his other epistles. Here is his prayer:

> For this reason I bow my knees before the Father, from whom every family in heaven and on earth is named, that according to the riches of his glory he may grant you to be strengthened with might through his Spirit in the inner [person], and that Christ may dwell in your hearts through faith; that you, being rooted and grounded in love, may have power to comprehend with all the saints what is the breadth and length and height and depth, and to know the love of Christ which surpasses knowledge, that you may be filled with all the fulness of God.
>
> Now to him who by the power at work within us is able to do far more abundantly than all that we ask or think, to him be

103

glory in the church and in Christ Jesus to all generations, for ever and ever. Amen (verses 14-21).

Dr. D. Martin Lloyd-Jones, the famed preacher and successor of Dr. G. Campbell Morgan at Westminster Chapel in London, devoted several years to the preaching of this letter of Paul. Chapter 3 alone took him one year—twenty-four sermons. His sermons on Ephesians are contained in five volumes, published by Baker Book House. The limited nature of this book prevents me from doing the same.

Two prayers contrasted

Paul begins by declaring, "I bow my knees before the Father." The normal Jewish position for prayer was standing. Kneeling represents a more spiritually intense appeal to God. This prayer contrasts with Paul's prayer in Ephesians 1, where he makes no reference to kneeling.

Both prayers deal with the same issue: the work that God has accomplished in Christ of bringing about unity in diversity among His people. However, the second prayer is more intense and more specific. Both refer to God as Father. The first calls God "the Father of glory"; the second stresses the fatherhood of God, "from whom every family in heaven and in earth is named." Paul means that every family, no matter where, is family with every other human family, because their common origin is from God's paternity. It is in this sense that Paul says in Acts 17:26, "He has made from one blood every nation" (NKJV). Here, then, is the concept of the unity of the human race because of creation. However, God has also made of *one blood* all nations through the blood of Jesus Christ. In this latter sense there is no New Testament doctrine of a universal fatherhood of God among the nations. While it is true that all humans have a common ancestry,[1] only through Christ do they truly become sons and daughters of God. Paul brings out the same truth in Galatians 4:4-7. Thus, there is a sense in which there are two fatherhoods of God: a general one through creation, made manifest through natural revelation and science; and a more specific one through redemption, made

104

manifest through special revelation and theology. The former signals the need of the latter; yet only through the latter is salvation possible.

Both prayers also refer to the gift of the Spirit, but again with different emphases. In the first prayer Paul asks that the Ephesians may understand the mystery that Jew and Gentile have been united in Christ. The second prayer is "for strength to grasp the mystery, to be rooted in love, and be filled up to the fulness of God."[2] The first prayer focused on the "eyes of the heart," the second on the "inner man," physically, mentally, spiritually, and socially. This latter prayer moves to a deeper level of communion and understanding of God's intention for the human family. The first prayer spoke of enlightenment, a gift from without. Strength, however, "comes from an indwelling power, making itself perfect in weakness, and continually growing from grace to grace."[3]

And what is that "indwelling power"? It is the second Person of the Trinity: "Christ in you, the hope of glory" (Colossians 1:27). Here is the fulfillment of Jesus' promise to His disciples, and to every disciple in every age: "I will not leave you orphans; I will come to you. . . . At that day you will know that I am in My Father, and you in Me, and I in you" (John 14:18, 20, NKJV). The function of the Spirit is to make Christ's dwelling in our hearts a living reality. "That Christ may dwell in your hearts through faith" (Ephesians 3:17). We must meditate on this phrase, saturating our minds with it until it becomes a living experience. Thus the children's chorus contains a most important gospel truth:

> Into my heart,
> Into my heart,
> Come into my heart,
> Lord Jesus;
> Come in today,
> Come in to stay,
> Come into my heart,
> Lord Jesus.

This is the gospel, pure and unadulterated, "That Christ may dwell in your hearts through faith."

Three consequences of the indwelling Christ

There are three consequences to Christ dwelling in the heart. The first is love. "Rooted and grounded in love" (verse 17). This is similar to the expression in Colossians 2:7, "Rooted and built up in him." "The idea in 'rooted' is of striking down deeper and spreading wider into the soil."[4] Normally the direction of growth is up, as in "built up" in Him. But here Paul speaks of growth downward, deeper and deeper, as we are "grounded" in Christ's love. Through the indwelling Christ, the Christian becomes rooted and grounded in love, which results in unity with God and with one another.

The second consequence of the indwelling Christ is the four-dimensional comprehension: "That you . . . may have power to comprehend with all the saints what is the breadth and length and height and depth" (Ephesians 3:17, 18). Breadth, length, height, and depth of what? Paul does not say. We normally assume that he means the love of Christ, and many translators and commentators so interpret the text. But that is a separate knowledge, as the original Greek brings out. "To know the love of Christ which surpasses knowledge" (verse 19). In harmony with the context of chapter 3, the focus of which is the "mystery of Christ"—"how the Gentiles are fellow heirs, members of the same body, and partakers of the promise in Christ Jesus through the gospel" (chap. 3:6)—Paul's prayer here is that we may know this mystery in all of its four dimensions. That we may comprehend its *breadth*—it encompasses every family in heaven and on earth (3:15); its *length*—this was God's plan before the foundation of the world (1:4); its *height*—it will even be made known to the principalities and powers in the heavenly places (3:10); and its *depth*—it reaches down to lowest levels of human helplessness, to those who are separated from Christ, alienated from the family, strangers to the promises, with no hope and without God in the world (2:12). Nothing is left out of God's mystery in Christ, and that is why we must comprehend it. And in comprehending it, we will come to know the love of Christ, which surpasses all human knowledge. Such love-action confounds the human mind, baffles human thought, and amazes the best of human action. The prophet Isaiah says, "My thoughts are not your thoughts, neither are your ways my ways, says the Lord. For as the heavens are higher than the earth, so are my ways higher than your ways and my thoughts than your thoughts" (Isaiah 55:8, 9). Ellen White declares, "Higher than the highest human thought can reach is God's ideal for His children."[5] That is love, surpassing all knowledge.

Notice that "the spiritual order of revelation differs from that of the 'wisdom of the world' [being its opposite]. It has first faith, next love, and finally knowledge, because its object is a person, not an abstract principle."[6]

The third consequence is the final and glorious climax of the plan of salvation—"that you may be filled with all the fulness of God" (verse 19). Paul states this more clearly in chapter 4:13: "Until we all attain to the unity of the faith and of the knowledge of the Son of God, to mature [personhood], to the measure of the stature of the fulness of Christ." He means perfect conformity to the image of Christ, in whom "the whole fulness of deity dwells bodily" (Colossians 2:9).

That's the beautiful, final, glorious climax awaiting every believer in Christ!

After such a climax, the only way Paul can close his prayer is with a doxology: "Now to Him who by the power at work within us is able to do far more abundantly than all that we ask or think, to him be glory in the church and in Christ Jesus to all generations, for ever and ever. Amen" (verses 20, 21). This doxology summarizes everything that has gone before. Alfred Barry declares, "In the parallelism of these clauses is implied the great idea of the Epistle—the unity of the Church in Christ. Hence all that is 'in the Church' is 'in Christ Jesus.' The visible unity of the church represents, as it depends on, the invisible unity of God in Him."[7]

The final phrase is mistranslated in the various versions of the Bible. It literally says, "To all the generations of the age of the ages." Each generation is to understand this mystery of

Christ; each generation is to manifest this mystery of unity in diversity in Christ; each generation is to add its own peculiar refrain of thanksgiving to the great, mighty chorus of praise, which will fill eternity with love. Ellen White declares:

> The years of eternity, as they roll, will bring richer and still more glorious revelations of God and of Christ. As knowledge is progressive, so will love, reverence, and happiness increase. The more [humans] learn of God, the greater will be their admiration of His character. As Jesus opens before them the riches of redemption and the amazing achievements in the great controversy with Satan, the hearts of the ransomed thrill with more fervent devotion, and with more rapturous joy they sweep the harps of gold; and ten thousand times ten thousand and thousands of thousands of voices unite to swell the mighty chorus of praise. . . .
>
> From the minutest atom to the greatest world, all things, animate and inanimate, in their unshadowed beauty and perfect joy, declare that God is love."[8]

---

1. Joseph A. Grassi, "The Letter to the Ephesians," in *The Jerome Biblical Commentary,* edited by Raymond E. Brown, Joseph A. Fitzmyer, and Roland E. Murphy (Englewood Cliffs, N.J.: Prentice-Hall, Inc., 1968), p. 346; see also the last chapter of this book, Addendum, "The Healing of the Nations."

2. Alfred Barry, "The Epistle to the Ephesians," in *Ellicott's Commentary on the Whole Bible,* edited by Charles John Ellicott (Grand Rapids, Mich.: Zondervan Publishing House, 1970), p. 35.

3. *Ibid.*

4. *Ibid.*

5. Ellen G. White, *Education* (Mountain View, Calif.: Pacific Press, 1903), p. 18.

6. Barry, p. 35.

7. *Ibid.,* p. 36.

8. Ellen G. White, *The Great Controversy* (Mountain View, Calif.: Pacific Press, 1911), p. 678.

Eleven

The Fatherhood of God

The central message of Paul's letter to the Ephesians is the truth that in Christ, all religious and social barriers have been broken down so that Christ might create one new humanity in place of many, thereby bringing peace. Unity in diversity in Christ is the theme. The locus—the center of activity where this unity is to be made manifest—is in the church, wherein the peace of God is to be made a living reality. This unity is not manifested in an ecclesiastical vacuum, however, but in living color, in the social context of our earthly experience—in other words, in the world.

Thus, the message of Ephesians is that young and old, male and female, and persons of every racial, cultural, and national background are included in the faith community. Basic to this sense of equality and inclusiveness in the community of faith—the church—is the recognition that God, by creation and redemption, is the Progenitor of all nations—the Father of the human race. And if God is our Father, then we are all sisters and brothers. In other words, at the heart of this new truth that Paul received through Christ and has made manifest to both Jew and Gentile is a new understanding of the nature of God—not only the concept of God as Father, but also of the redeemed as family:

There is one body and one Spirit, just as you were called to the one hope that belongs to your call, one Lord, one faith, one baptism, one God and Father of us all, who is above all and through all and in all (Ephesians 4:4-6).

God as Father:

In the Old Testament God is referred to as Father only fifteen times.[1] Father was not a common expression by which to address God. It was used primarily as a reference to God's relationship to the nation of Israel.

For the Jew, God's name *YHWH* was so holy that they would not even utter it. Instead, they used the term *Adonai,* meaning "Lord," or *Elohim,* meaning "God." Or they simply referred to heaven, where God dwells. Thus Matthew, in respect for his Jewish audience, refers often to the kingdom of "heaven" as an expression for the kingdom of "God." Nowhere in ancient literature did the Jews use the expression "my Father" as a personal form of address to God—not even in prayer.[2] For them, God was too transcendent, too remote and removed. They could not address Him in such a manner.

Of course, Jesus knew all this. Yet the surprising thing is that He never addressed God in any form *other* than the Aramaic word *Abba.* This childlike expression is derived from baby talk, the first babbling sounds a child makes in recognition of its father—*abba,* meaning "daddy." It was a familial term by which not only infants but also older children and even adults addressed their parents, much the same as today when children progress from the infant expression of "dadda" to "Daddy" to "Dad." It suggests intimacy, oneness, warmth, and accessibility. Not everyone can address another person as "Daddy," but only those who are part of the family, who are sons and daughters, who have a close, intimate relationship with their father. "It must have seemed nothing short of outrageous that Jesus should make use of the completely unceremonious Aramaic word *abba* as an expression to address God."[3] Jesus literally surprised His hearers with His manner of praying and addressing God in prayer.

We must keep in mind that Jesus came from a people who knew how to pray. Three times a day, devout Jews stopped everything and prayed. But their prayers were ritualistic, done by rote, to a God who was removed. Jesus brought His disciples a whole new understanding of prayer. As Joachim Jeremias says, with Jesus, "a new way of praying is born. Jesus talks to His father as naturally, as intimately and with the same sense of security as a child talks to his father."[4]

Jesus' mode of praying reflected His special relationship to God. It wasn't formal prayer worked into a ritual, but a personal, intimate style, similar to a child speaking with his father. This greatly impressed the disciples. When they asked Jesus, "Teach us to pray" (Luke 11:1), they were not asking for the basic how-to of praying, for they already knew that. They wanted to know *how to pray as Jesus prayed.* Something about the way He prayed moved them, especially the close, intimate manner in which He addressed God. They wanted the same close relationship with God. Jesus replied by giving them the Lord's Prayer, in which He authorized His disciples also to address God as *abba,* "Daddy," "Our Father," thereby giving them "a share in His relationship to God."[5] In telling us to pray, "Our Daddy, who is in heaven," Jesus gives His disciples:

> a share in His sonship and empowers them, as His disciples, to speak with their heavenly Father in just such a familiar, trusting way as a child would with his father. Yes, He goes so far as to say that it is this new relationship which first opens the doors to God's reign: "Truly, I say to you, unless you become like children again, you will not find entrance into the kingdom of God" (Matt. 18:3). Children can say *abba!*
>
> Only he who, through Jesus, lets himself be given the childlike trust which resides in the word *abba* finds his way into the kingdom of God. This the apostle Paul also understood; he says twice that there is no surer sign or guarantee of the possession of the Holy Spirit and of the gift of sonship than this, that a [person] makes bold to repeat this one word, Abba, dear Father (Rom. 8:15; Gal. 4:6).[6]

111

The early church followed Jesus in addressing God as "Daddy," *abba,* and even admonished us to do so (see Romans 8:15, 16 and Galatians 4:6). This concept of God as *abba,* Daddy, lies behind Paul's expression in Ephesians 4:6, "One God and Father [Daddy] of us all."

Jesus gives us a new understanding of God—not the distant, detached, and disinterested God of Judaism, but the intimate, incarnate, involved God of Jesus Christ. This is the God we are to address as "Daddy," "Father."

If some today have difficulty with such a familiar approach to God, imagine how people in Jesus' day must have felt, when they were told to do likewise in the Lord's Prayer! Jesus radically altered people's understanding of God. His whole approach was most revolutionary. He broke loose the bonds of a patriarchal understanding of God as Lord, Master, King, and Fearful One, and gave His followers a new vision of God as an intimate, caring, compassionate Daddy, accessible to His children. "As a father pities his children, so the Lord pities those who fear him" (Psalm 103:13).

God revealed an understanding of His nature to His people according to their need and reflective of their age and society. In Old Testament times, in the midst of a strongly patriarchal society, God allowed Himself to be revealed in patriarchal imagery. At the time of Christ, when God wanted to reveal His closeness to the human family, He revealed Himself as a child crying, "Dadda," "Daddy." Today, in the new information age of satellite communications, the world has been turned into a small global village where we share each other's hurts and where the needs of the neglected and the despised are now made prominent. In this context God desires to be revealed in imagery inclusive of the whole human family, both male and female, and reflective of God's entire being.

Let me state this another way. Take Paul's famous text in Galatians 3:28, "There is neither Jew nor Greek, . . . slave nor free, . . . male nor female; for you are all one in Christ Jesus." In the first century the church had to come to grips with the first line, the conflict between Jew and Gentile, and addressed a new understanding of God reflective of that new experience.

That is what the entire letter to the Ephesians is about. Paul uses the concept of Father eleven times in this letter—more than in any other of his epistles. The gospel demands a new relationship between Jew and Gentile, at the heart of which is a new understanding of God as the common Father of humankind, especially redeemed humanity. This, in turn, results in a new humanity in Christ—one that experiences oneness with its Saviour and with each other, because all are family. Thus Paul declares in Ephesians 3:14, 15, "I bow my knees before the Father, from whom every family in heaven and on earth is named."

In the nineteenth century the Christian church had to wage war with the second line, proclaiming that human slavery was inconsistent with the Christian faith. During this time the majority of those countries that practiced slavery brought the practice to an end. This was due to a new understanding of God. They now understood that God was against oppression in all its forms. The Negro spiritual conveyed this new understanding of God in subtle language: "Go down, Moses. Tell ol' Pharaoh, way down in Egypt's land, Let my people go!"

In the twentieth century we wrestle with the third line of the trilogy: "There is neither male nor female." The world is ahead of the church in this matter, but the church has a greater motivating force, the power of the gospel.[7] God is revealing a new understanding of Himself to the church, and through the church to the world. In an age of global oppression, we need to grasp a more inclusive understanding of God as a compassionate, caring Being who, like a mother, cares for her children. There really is no such thing as "Mother Nature," for Mother Nature is God.

Are we saying that God is now a woman? No! No more than that God is a man.

By thinking of God in these inclusive ways, we lift the burden of oppression from those who have been at the receiving end of dehumanizing action. Can you imagine how the women in Jesus' day must have felt when He included them in His conversations, His illustrations, His sermons, His actions, and treated them as intelligent human beings, equal to men?

113

No wonder Fanny J. Crosby declares,

A wonderful Saviour is Jesus my Lord,
He taketh my burden away,
He holdeth me up, and I shall not be moved,
He giveth me strength as my day.

The mission of the church is to do likewise. Will it be faithful?

---

1. O. Hofius, "Father," in *The New International Dictionary of New Testament Theology,* edited by Colin Brown (Grand Rapids, Mich.: Zondervan, 1975), vol. 1, p. 617.

2. Joachim Jeremias, *The Prayers of Jesus* (Naperville, Ill.: A. R. Allenson, Inc., 1967), p. 29.

3. Hofius, p. 620.

4. Jeremias, p. 78.

5. *Ibid.,* p. 63.

6. *Ibid.,* pp. 97, 98.

7. See Caleb Rosado, *Women: Their Role in the Church and the Nature of God—A Socio-biblical Study* (Riverside, Calif.: Loma Linda University Press, 1989).

Twelve

Unity Does Not Mean Uniformity

Paul's letter to the Ephesians is divided into two parts. Part one is his basic theology of unity in Christ, which transcends all social divisions. Part two deals with the practical outworking of unity in the church. Chapters 1 to 3 focus on the great mystery of God's saving plan for humankind. God intends to bring unity in all things in order to remove all hostile divisions, all social barriers, all religious stalemates that maintain separations between peoples of different cultures. This unity is to be made manifest in the church, the body of Christ. Obviously, if the church is Christ's body, its attitudes and actions must be congruent with its "Head," who is Christ. If the body behaves differently from the Head, then it must belong to a different head.

The second part of Ephesians, chapters 4 to 6, discusses the practical outworking of this theology in the Christian's life. This is first seen in the division of responsibilities in the church, then in the loving concern of Christians for each other, and finally in family relationships. The letter closes with instructions on how to be spiritually suited for battle against the biggest foe of this unity, the powers of darkness.

A sevenfold statement of unity

Paul begins the second section with a call to humility, patience, and tolerance (chap. 4:1, 2). In these three character qualities we have the greatest statement on human relations across racial and gender lines that the church has ever received. In Colossians 3:12-16 we have the same three words, introduced by two key Christian concepts—compassion and kindness.

Notice the context of this compassion, kindness, humility, meekness, and patience, as stated in verse 11: "Here there cannot be Greek and Jew, circumcised and uncircumcised, barbarian, Scythian, slave, free man, but Christ is all, and in all." This is the same idea expressed in Galatians 3:28.

These three qualities—humility, patience, tolerance—correspond with the first, third, and fifth Beatitudes of the Sermon on the Mount, which are really "beautiful attitudes" (see Matthew 5).

1. "Blessed are the poor in spirit" (verse 3)—those who humble themselves.

2. "Blessed are the meek" (verse 5)—the gentle, who keep their cool when others are losing theirs.

3. "Blessed are the merciful" (verse 7)—the compassionate, those who have tolerance for others.

The goal of these Christian character qualities is found in Ephesians 4:3: "Eager to maintain the unity of the Spirit in the bond of peace."

Why should the Christian live by these qualities? The answer is found in the sevenfold statement of unity (verses 4-6). "Each of the seven expressions brings out an aspect of the basic unity."[1] One body—one external, visible community; one Spirit—one single inner source; one hope—one future, unified community in glory; one Lord—one Master; one faith—one fixed body of beliefs; one baptism—one initiation rite; one God who is *abba*—our one and only Daddy, our Father.

Is there any greater reason for unity in the church than this sevenfold unity? Everything about the Christian's collective life should spell *unity* and *oneness!*

The gifts of the Spirit

But this unity does not mean uniformity. Each member must contribute in his or her own unique way to the growth and progress of the church. If we could only understand the truth of this principle, we would not fall into the trap of *ethnocentrism*.

Most of us suffer from the social "disease" of cultural myopia—the tendency to view members of other ethnic groups negatively due to a nearsighted field of cultural vision, where the world as we know it is seen exclusively from the perspective of our own ethnic viewpoint. Such nearsightedness results in ethnocentrism—the attitude whereby "one's own group is the center of everything, and all others are scaled and rated with reference to it."[2] Though ethnocentrism is generally a positive concept that enables a people to establish their place in history, it also serves as a means to view other groups negatively. Thus, one's own group becomes the standard by which all other groups are judged, and, since groups differ, others are regarded as inferior. Such a myopic view fails to appreciate the ideas of others and is not able to recognize the commonality of humanity. This is because groups tend to be farsighted with regard to themselves, but nearsighted when it comes to others.

Besides its impact on intercultural relations, ethnocentrism also impacts the church in two additional ways—structurally and socially. The group in power demands and dictates the ways of doing things: how to carry on the work of the church, how to dress, how to organize the structure, how to establish an institutional presence so that it will be according to the dominant standards and ways of social organization. The result is a cultural imposition on the rest of the world body.

While it is true that certain basic principles of Christian action and ways of doing things transcend culture, the gospel allows for much more latitude than the church is often willing to allow. The danger in the church is that of making the American cultural value system prominent, as though it were synonymous with the divine will, and regarding it as the "Christian" manner of conduct for Christians worldwide. The result

117

of such policies is uniformity, which our very passage of Scripture negates.

Three passages of Scripture deal with spiritual gifts: Romans 12:3 to 9; 1 Corinthians 12:1 to 31; and Ephesians 4:11 to 15. All three differ. In Ephesians the focus is on the church, and not on individual Christians, as in the other two passages. In 1 Corinthians the focus is on "a 'horizontal' picture of the body of Christ; Head, hands, feet, all refer to Christians having various gifts due to the working of one Spirit in all. In Ephesians it is a 'vertical' picture: Christ is the head, the vitalizing, unifying force of the body whose members are joined to Him."[3]

The Godhead is involved in all three. God is the source of the gifts in Romans. In Corinthians the Spirit is the source. In Ephesians the source is the risen Christ.

The purpose of the gifts is found in Ephesians 4:12: "To equip the saints for the work of the ministry, for building up the body of Christ." The goal is seen in verse 13 and the following verses: "That we may no longer be children." "The work of Christ in the Church is not primarily to find people who are already mature and responsible, but to bring people to maturity who through weakness are as 'children.'"[4] Verses 15 and 16 emphasize what happens to the church when all members exercise their gifts, not according to human dictation and demand, but according to the Spirit's.

The key unifying concept is *love.* "It is the acting directive force behind the gifts."[5] This is why Paul in Corinthians follows his chapter on spiritual gifts with a chapter on love. Love moves Christians to exercise their gifts to build up others in the community of faith rather than to edify themselves.[6]

Our cultural richness

The Christian church is a diverse body of believers united in Christ. The richness of this diversity makes for the church's "body beautiful."

According to the *Harvard Encyclopedia of American Ethnic Groups,* there are some 106 identifiable ethnic groups in the United States of America, including 173 native American Indian nations that can be further subdivided into 500 tribal groups, all subsumed under one group called "American Indian." By contrast, the Seventh-day Adventist Church has an institutional presence in over 180 countries throughout the world. This rich cultural mix of people gives Adventists their uniqueness in the religious world, for Adventists are one of the few "world" churches. The majority of our membership is outside the United States, in contrast to most Protestant groups in the United States whose dominant presence is in the U.S., with only a small percentage in the rest of the world. Like the United States, the Seventh-day Adventist Church is comprised of many nations.

In their latest book, *Re-Inventing the Corporation,* John Naisbett and Patricia Aburdene contrast the difference between American and Japanese societies. They make a most important and crucial point, which is applicable to the mission of the Seventh-day Adventist Church.

> The Japanese have a long way to go before beating the United States in the information revolution. The Japanese have one culture, one history, one race. Superb as they are, that is a limiting factor. They are very good at hardware, but the United States is better at software, at thoughtware. This is because the United States has the richest mix of ethnic groups and races the world has ever known. The richer the mix, the more the creativity. It is not by chance that the United States has won 125 Nobel prizes and Japan has won only 2.
>
> In the United States, we have not yet begun to develop the real potential of our fantastic mix of people, our real competitive edge in the global market.[7]

Neither have Seventh-day Adventists. In an information age of cultural diversity and pluralism, we are still pushing the industrial society's assembly-line model of uniformity, operating on the basis of homogeneous models of ministry within a heterogeneous world society.

Naisbett concludes: "To reach our full potential as individuals, as companies, as a country, though, we need a vision."

So does the church, for long ago the wise man declared,

119

"Without vision a people perish" (author's paraphrase of Proverbs 29:18). We need a vision relevant to the needs of a changing society. The play *Inherit the Wind* by Jerome Lawrence and Robert E. Lee is a dramatization of the famous Scope's trial over creation and evolution. In the play the prosecuting attorney, Matthew Brady, asks his old friend Henry Drummond, the defense attorney, why he has moved so far away from him in his orientation toward life. "No," responds Drummond, "all motion is relative. Maybe it is you who have moved away . . . by standing still."

Can the same be said of the church in relation to society? Has the church stood still, while society has moved with time? To stay relevant, the church must not only respond to change; it must also *anticipate* change, for change challenges leadership to deal more effectively with differences.

As a nation we have moved from an agrarian society concerned with conformity, through an industrial society concerned with nationalism and uniformity, to an international information society concerned with cultural diversity within a global village.[8] In this new information society, with its global worldview, the focus is on diversity and *cultural pluralism*. With this new global outlook needs to come a new way of perceiving the world and a new model of ministry—global and multicultural in nature. We must be sensitive to the leading of the Spirit in our individual and institutional life and thus make the church safe for cultural differences.

Music for the worship of God is a good example. Because of their European heritage, many White Western Christians have come to accept as the norm for worship that liturgical form known as "high church." High church worship includes traditional music—the hymns of Watts and Wesley—and the piano and pipe organ as the principle musical instruments. Other groups, arising out of a different cultural heritage, approach the worship experience with music reflective of their suffering and liberation from oppression, accompanied by instruments derived from their society, which may include guitars, tambourines, and drums, but not pianos and organs. However, the tendency is for the dominant group that holds power in the church to see itself as the channel through which God communicates the faith to other cultures, and to view its forms of worship as normative for all. Yet both forms of worship, and those that fall in between, are legitimate expressions of praise to God, for God speaks to humanity where it is found. In the sense, then, that each style arises out of the religious experience of a particular group of worshipers and meets the needs of that group, each style is an acceptable form of worship, though not necessarily the only way to worship.

God does not want uniformity in the church, but only unity—unity in diversity in Christ. The result will be a world family fellowshiping in the unity of the faith.

1. Joseph A. Grassi, "The Letter to the Ephesians," in *The Jerome Biblical Commentary,* edited by Raymond E. Brown, Jospeh A. Fitzmyer and Roland E. Murphy (Englewood Cliffs, N.J.: Prentice-Hall, Inc., 1968), p. 347.

2. William Graham Sumner, *Folkways and Mores* (New York: Schocken Books, 1979), p. 13.

3. Grassi, p. 347.

4. *Ibid.*

5. *Ibid.*

6. *Ibid.*

7. John Naisbett and Patricia Aburdene, *Re-Inventing the Corporation* (New York: Warner Books, 1985), p. 255.

8. For a fuller explanation of this shift in societies, see the article by Caleb Rosado, "The Nature of Society and the Challenge to the Mission of the Church," *International Review of Mission* 77:305 (January 1988), pp. 22-37.

Thirteen

Morals and Lifestyle in the Church

One of the most problematic areas for the church is that of lifestyle standards: what constitutes appropriate and inappropriate behavior for the Christian. Unfortunately, discussion in this area by Christians has generated more heat than light. The apostle Paul, in section two of his letter, addresses this problem of standards, but he approaches the subject from a perspective seldom taken into consideration by Christians in their discussion of the practical outgrowth of the gospel for daily living.

Paul begins the section with one word: humility. "I therefore, a prisoner for the Lord, beg you to lead a life worthy of the calling to which you have been called, with all [humility] and meekness, with patience, forbearing one another in love" (4:1, 2). Why does Paul begin the exhortation section on the practice of Christian unity with the concept of humility? I believe it is because pride, the very opposite of humility, "is the prime source of Christian disunity."[1] Ellen White declares, "There is nothing so offensive to God or so dangerous to the human soul as pride and self-sufficiency. Of all sins it is the most hopeless, the most incurable."[2] Why? Because pride knows no need. And the worst form of pride is *racial* pride. I submit to you that the leading problem in society and in the church today is this problem of racial pride. Every other problem or difficulty in the church pales in the presence of this one.

It was the leading problem in the early church, creating conflict between Jew and Gentile. In the Middle Ages it was the problem that launched the Crusades, as Christian Europe did not want the dark-skinned Moors to control the Holy Land. It was the basic philosophy that legitimized Europe's exploitation of nonwestern peoples in the sixteenth century. It was the instigator of the uprooting of more than 100 million Africans from their homeland, forcing them to become machines in the new world's pre-industrial society. It was the ideology behind Hitler's Third Reich, his obsession for developing a supreme race, and the annihilation of six million Jews in the Holocaust. It is the force that divides the world into First World and Third World, for one is primarily White and the other primarily Black. And today, it is the principal concept on which the nation of South Africa is structured. It has given rise in the United States to neo-Nazi groups, skinheads, and racial supremacists—the concept of the racial superiority of Whites and the racial inferiority of all others.

In addressing the subject of the lifestyle standards of the church, we must realize that the church's greatest moral problem—racial pride—has yet to be included in its list of standards, the violation of which are regarded as tests of fellowship. We disfellowship people for problems with alcohol, tobacco, adultery, theft, Sabbath breaking, etc., but not for racial discrimination.

Yet Jesus declared that the two great commandments were to love God with all our heart, soul, and mind; and our neighbor as ourselves. On these two commandments, He declared, depend *all* the law and the prophets (see Matthew 22:37-40). Everything in Scripture depends on my love for God and love for my fellow human beings.

The problem with moral standards

Ephesians 4:17 to 5:20 forms a thematic unit that deals

with moral standards. The entire section abounds with rich, meaningful phrases.

Two principal points need to be understood about Paul's message in this section. These two points form the central core of the section. We could spend much time with each verse in the section and focus on all the moral concerns contained therein and still not come to grips with these two central truths. In fact, this is the main problem in the way the church has taught its lifestyle standards, and why, if Christians fail in one area, it tends to be in this area of lifestyle. In transmitting our lifestyle standards from one generation to the next, we have taught them without these two essential points.

The result has been meaningless standards. Each generation is in conflict with the previous generation over what is appropriate or inappropriate behavior. Conflicts in the church between generations usually have to do with lifestyle, because what each generation considers to be appropriate Christian behavior tends to be tied to what that generation values in its social context. Since social contexts change constantly, social standards also tend to be in a continual state of flux. Thus, what is considered wrong by one generation in its social context may be perfectly acceptable to another generation in a different social context.

Let me illustrate. In Cuba a Seventh-day Adventist will be disfellowshiped for wearing jeans—any kind of jeans. That was a position the church held in the early 1950s. Since Cuba, in many ways, is a society frozen in pre-1960 times, it still adheres to a pre-sixties "moral" standard. However, Cubans who emigrate to the United States soon find themselves wearing jeans. Lest some be too hasty in passing judgment on the Cubans, let me remind you that many Adventist grade schools in the United States do not permit the wearing of blue denim jeans to school, nor do many of our academies. Children can wear red jeans, white jeans, green jeans, but not blue jeans. Yet youth in our colleges and universities can wear them, and that is a most confusing norm for Adventist youth and children. What is wrong with the color *blue?* Our children can see through the phoniness of that standard faster than church leaders and school administrators can blink an eye.

Years ago, in the book *Child Guidance,* Ellen White gave guiding principles for the purchase of clothing for children.

1. It must be of *durable* material (CH 107).
2. It must be *warm* (CG 425).
3. It must have *simple* lines (CG 107).
4. It must be *inexpensive* [does this rule out designer clothes?] (CG 141).
5. It should require little work to *wash* and *iron* (CG 462).

What she describes here appears to be denim jeans. *Webster's Third International Dictionary* defines *denim* as "firm durable twilled usually cotton fabric woven with colored warp and white filling threads." Thus, denim is one of the warmer cotton fabrics, which means that the very thing Ellen White recommends is what Adventist school administrators most object to in children's clothes. Very interesting!

The result is a twofold tragedy: we raise an issue that has nothing to do with morality to the level of a moral issue, and in so doing we lower the moral value of those issues that are of serious moral concern. To put it another way, we make something out to be sin that has nothing to do with sin. In either case the church loses, and the moral value of the Christian life is lowered. The result is a moral tragedy, for morality issues are now confused in the minds of our youth.

If we don't stop letting our narrow, negative values determine our moral standards, we will turn out a generation with few standards except those enforced by the law of punishment.

The two central principles

What are the two central principles of Ephesians 4:17 to 5:20 that should govern our understanding of the moral standards of the church?

The first one is: *God is our moral standard.* Not some external rule; not some contrived and contradictory handbook policy, but God. God is the example of Christian moral conduct (verses 4:32; 5:1). The problem we have here is that chapter divisions are artificial and sometimes break up the writer's meaning. Chapter 5:1, which calls on Christians to be imitators of God, is immediately preceded by chapter 4:32, which calls on them to imitate God's forgiveness. Notice how the New English Bible states it:

> Be generous to one another, tender-hearted, forgiving one another as God in Christ forgave you. In a word, as God's dear children, try to be like him, and live in love as Christ loved you, and gave himself up on your behalf as an offering and sacrifice whose fragrance is pleasing to God.

God is our standard of conduct. If we would only remember that, it would save us a great deal of headache over what to do in a given situation.

The second principle Paul makes in this passage on moral standards is that *the reason for our moral behavior is others, not ourselves.* The passage begins by declaring, "This I affirm and testify in the Lord, that you must no longer live as the Gentiles do" (verse 17). How did the Gentiles live in Paul's day? They lived for themselves (verses 17-19). Their selfish living concerned itself with the gratification of the flesh. This is the way the "old man," the old nature, lives. This "old man" concept denotes the life we led before knowing Christ, with merely the resources belonging to human nature as sons and daughters of Adam and Eve.[3]

Paul then declares: "You did not so learn Christ!" "Put on the new nature, created after the likeness of God in true righteousness and holiness" (verses 20, 24). "The 'new Man' refers to incorporation into Christ Himself, the new Adam, the head of a renewed humanity sharing His Spirit. It connotes the attainment of all that human beings were intended to be when God first made Adam and Eve according to His image." [4] The difference between the Gentile and the Christian is that the Christian, like his moral Standard of behavior—Christ—lives, like Christ, for others. "Walk in love, as Christ loved us and gave himself up for us" (verse 5:2).

Notice the number of times Paul connects our moral behavior with others in chapter 4:

1. Verse 25: We are to put away lying, for it affects others to whom we are intimately related in Christ.

2. Verse 26: Anger affects others; therefore, "be sure that it is not out of wounded pride or bad temper" (Phillips).

3. Verse 27: "Don't give the devil that sort of foothold" (Phillips). The "other" can even be the devil, giving him an opportunity for advantage over us.

4. Verse 28: The thief must not steal, for stealing is taking away from others. Instead let him work so that he can give to others in need.

5. Verse 29: Use no foul language, for it does not edify others, but good language that "may impart grace to those who hear."

6. Verse 30: Such conduct grieves another—the Holy Spirit, who is the "personal pledge of your eventual full redemption" (Phillips).

7. Verse 31: "Let all bitterness and wrath and anger and clamor and slander be put away from you, with all malice."

This long list is of actions that affect others. What should we do then? Verse 32 says that our actions toward others must nurture them in love. "Be kind to one another, tenderhearted, forgiving one another." This is what Ellen White said: "If we would humble ourselves before God, and be kind and courteous and tenderhearted and pitiful, there would be one hundred conversions to the truth where now there is only one."[5]

What is our moral standard of conduct? "As God in Christ forgave you" (verse 32). God is the moral Standard of the church. Understanding this enables us to walk in the Spirit.

Thus, as Joseph A. Grassi says, "It is no longer a question of right and wrong; it is a matter of respect for brothers and sisters in Christ and a realization of how our actions can affect them."[6] The central focus of the moral standards of the church is others, not ourselves.

In an urban, secular context, where people care little whether you wear blue jeans or white jeans, our concern must be with the greater moral standard: *Love your neighbor as yourself*! For such people, racial discrimination is a far greater moral offense than wearing blue denim jeans! Yet for people concerned with blue jeans, racial discrimination is not seen as sin at all, but as a way of protecting their petty values, because the focus of their moral standards is on themselves and not on others. Thus, it is possible to be a Christian—or at least claim to be a Christian—and yet live like Gentiles, with our focus on ourselves.

To such practicing Christians Ellen White addressed the next line of her famous "tenderhearted" statement: "Though professing to be converted, we carry around with us a bundle of self that we regard as altogether too precious to be given up."[7] A "bundle of self"—pride! As stated previously, this statement was made in the context of *racial* pride and discrimination between the Germans and the Swedes in the Central Union Conference during the early 1900s. The beginnings of this movement can be traced to the separate facilities that were established at Union College in the early 1890s—a plan that seemed innocent enough at the time, but which bore fruit as racial conflict among adult Christians fifteen years later.

If this principle applied back then, how much more does it apply in today's culturally diverse church!

Conclusion

Is our standard of behavior some external rule of conduct or Christ? Is the focus of our ethical, moral behavior ourselves or others? Do we teach our children proper moral behavior for their own good or that of others? Do we teach them that Christ is their moral Standard, or do we teach them irrelevant rules that are meaningless in today's social context? The difference that the two central points of this passage make can be the difference between a relevant ministry to others or a selfish navel-gazing focus on ourselves.

The hymnwriter declares:

> I would be true, for there are those who trust me;
> I would be pure, for there are those who care;
> I would be strong, for there is much to suffer;

I would be brave, for there is much to dare;
I would be brave, for there is much to dare.

Let us be true for God, for He is the One who trusts us.

---

1. Henry Chadwick, "Ephesians," *Peake's Commentary on the Bible,* edited by Matthew Black and H. H. Rowley (London: Thomas Nelson and Sons, Ltd., 1962), p. 984.

2. Ellen G. White, *Christ's Object Lessons* (Washington, D.C.: Review and Herald, 1900), p. 154.

3. Joseph A. Grassi, "The Letter to the Ephesians," *The Jerome Biblical Commentary,* edited by Raymond E. Brown, Joseph A. Fitzmyer, and Roland E. Murphy (Englewood Cliffs, N.J.: Prentice-Hall, Inc., 1968), p. 347.

4. *Ibid.,* p. 348.

5. Ellen G. White, *Testimonies for the Church* (Mountain View, Calif.: Pacific Press, 1948), vol. 9, p. 189.

6. Grassi, p. 348.

7. White, *Testimonies*, p. 189.

129

Fourteen

Is the Head of the House at Home?

Recent discussions in the church have generated a lot of heat but very little light on the subject of the relationship of women to men in ministry and in the home.

Some maintain the traditional position that women are subordinate to men, based on the divine order of creation in which man was created first and woman was taken from man.[1] Others claim that this order of relationship is a product of sin, since the creation account holds both to be equal. Only after the Fall is one made subordinate to the other.[2] But through Christ the oneness prior to the Fall is restored. As a result, "there is neither Jew nor Greek, there is neither slave nor free, there is neither male nor female; for *you are all one in Christ Jesus*" (Galatians 3:28, emphasis supplied).

Both of these views seek to clarify the concept of "headship." One stresses that man is the head of the home; the other that headship does not mean lording it over the other. The problem is that both views focus on the human dimension of the relationship instead of the divine. As a result Christ, the moral Standard of conduct, is lost sight of.

The theme is unity

Through the ages men have appealed to Ephesians 5:21 to 23 to legitimize their dominance over women in domestic and church relations. Unfortunately, they divorced the passage from the central theme of the letter—unity in diversity. Christ has formed a new community that erased the social and religious barriers that divide the human family. The representation of this new community is the church—the new humanity in Christ—which exemplifies Christ's oneness in the members' behavior toward each other.

The world does not form this new humanity, for the world does not know God. This new humanity is to be made visible in the church, for it *is* the church! There are no differences based on race, for "there is neither Jew nor Greek"; there are no differences based on class, for "there is neither slave nor free"; neither are there differences based on gender, for "there is neither male nor female." Why? Because "you are all one in Christ Jesus" (Galatians 3:28).

In Ephesians 5:21 to 23, so often cited by those who seek to maintain the subordinate status of women, Paul tells us that this new humanity in Christ is to be made manifest in domestic relations as well, for Christian unity often falls apart in the relationship between husband and wife, parents and children, masters and slaves (though we no longer have the latter). As with relations between Jew and Gentile, so with domestic relations: they are no longer governed by social proprieties that divide and differentiate. So also with the church, the real subject of the passage: "This is a great mystery: but I speak concerning Christ and the church" (chap. 5:32, KJV). Both the Christian household and the Christian church must reflect the oneness brought about by Christ's saving act.

> He is our peace, who has made us both one, and has broken down the dividing wall of hostility, by abolishing in his flesh the law of commandments and ordinances [those rules and regulations that divide and differentiate between peoples], that he might create in himself one new [person] in place of the two, so making peace, and might reconcile us both [not just Jew and

Gentile, not just slave and free, but also male and female] to God in one body through the cross, thereby bringing the hostility to an end. And he came and preached peace to you who were far off and peace to those who were near; for through him we both [Jew and Gentile, male and female] have access in one Spirit to the Father. So then you are no longer strangers and sojourners, but you are fellow citizens with the saints and members of the household of God, built upon the foundation of the apostles and prophets, Christ Jesus himself being the cornerstone, in whom the whole structure [the church and the home] is joined together and grows into a holy temple in the Lord; in whom you also are built into it for a dwelling place of God in the Spirit (Ephesians 2:14-22).

Paul means that what is true in the household of God—the members of that household are one and equal in Christ—must also be true in our own households.

Unity in the home

Let us consider this passage in light of Paul's theme of unity. Ephesians is divided into two parts: God's plan for His church (chapters 1-3) and the practice of that plan in the church and in the home (chapters 4-6:9). Part two, the practical portion, begins with the idea of humility:

I therefore, a prisoner for the Lord, beg you to lead a life worthy of the calling to which you have been called, with all lowliness and meekness, with patience, forbearing one another in love, eager to maintain the unity of the Spirit in the bond of peace (4:1-3).

Why does Paul begin the exhortation section on the practice of Christian unity with the concept of humility? Because pride, the opposite of humility, "is the prime source of Christian disunity."[3] Along with racial pride stands sexual pride—the two worst forms of pride.

That is why Paul begins with humility. This virtue is the undergirding principle of the passage on domestic relations. Ephesians 5:21 says, "Be subject to one another out of reverence for Christ." This principle is to govern all domestic relations. As Henry Chadwick says, "The primacy of humility means that Christian marriage is a relation of mutual giving and subordination,"[4] first to Christ, and then to one another.

The expression "out of reverence for Christ" suggests that "Christ's self-sacrificing love for others (5:1) is now the model for home life."[5] Throughout this section the model for both wife and husband is Christ (verses 22, 25). "This presentation of Christ's love for the Church as a model for married love is unique to the NT."[6] The basis is Galatians 2:20. Ephesians 5:25 is an outgrowth of 5:1, 2: "Be imitators of God, as beloved children. And walk in love, as Christ loved us and gave himself up for us, a fragrant offering and sacrifice to God."

> The Christian is invited to make his life a sacrifice of love for others like that of Christ. When husband and wife do this by subjection and love, or mutual self-giving, then their married love will be a visible sign that they are imitating and sharing this invisible action of Christ.[7]

That's what it means to be the "head," not in authority, for Christ never lords it over the church, but in saving, self-sacrificing love (verses 25, 29). According to this passage, any man who fails to demonstrate that standard of love, yet demands that his wife obey and respect him out of his own self-interest, has no right to claim headship. Jesus does not demand our love and obedience. He has earned it. Love and obedience cannot be forced. They can only be earned.

The same holds true in parents' relation to their children. Here headship also means an example of self-sacrificing love (chap. 6:4). Again, the Lord is the example.

This relationship of love and mutual surrender between husband and wife is a human object lesson of Christ's relationship with His church. " 'For this reason a man shall leave his father and mother and be joined to his wife, and the two shall become one flesh.' This is a great mystery, but I speak concerning Christ and the church" (chap. 5:31, 32, NKJV).

The word *mystery* in Paul's writings signifies God's long-hidden secret. This means that the text in Genesis that Paul quotes has a hidden meaning that has now been brought to light: that the union between husband and wife symbolizes the union between Christ and the church—a union of oneness and personal fulfillment for both parties. Without that union, neither party is fulfilled—neither Jew nor Gentile, neither husband nor wife, neither Christ nor the church.

Conclusion

Is the head of the house at home? That salesman's question refers not to the husband but to Christ, the real Head of the home. Only where self-sacrificing love is made manifest can we dare to speak of the Head of the house being at home.

Thus, the old hymn writer is correct:

> Happy the home where God is there,
> And love fills every breast;
> When one their wish, and one their prayer
> And one their heavenly rest.[8]

1. Samuele Bacchiocchi, *Women in the Church* (Berrien Springs, Mich.: Biblical Perspectives, 1987).

2. Gerhard F. Hasel, "Equality From the Start: Woman in the Creation Story," *Spectrum* 7:2, pp. 21-28; Richard M. Davidson, "The Theology of Sexuality in the Beginning: Genesis 1-2," *Andrews University Seminary Studies* 26:1 (Spring 1988); and part 2 by the same author, "The Theology of Sexuality in the Beginning: Genesis 3," *Andrews University Seminary Studies* 26:2 (Summer 1988).

3. Henry Chadwick, "Ephesians," *Peake's Commentary on the Bible* edited by Matthew Black and H. H. Rowley (London: Thomas Nelson and Sons, Ltd., 1962), p. 984.

4. *Ibid.*

5. Joseph A. Grassi, "The Letter to the Ephesians," in *The Jerome Biblical Commentary,* edited by Raymond E. Brown, Joseph A. Fitzmyer, and Roland E. Murphy (Englewood Cliffs, N.J.: Prentice-Hall, Inc., 1968), p. 348.

6. *Ibid.*

7. *Ibid.,* p. 349.

8. Henry Ware, the younger (1794-1843).

Fifteen

Armed for the Struggle

We now come to the final section of Ephesians. The sixteen chapters of this book fall short of an exhaustive study of the letter. That would require a much larger book. We have been selective, seeking to bring forth those aspects of the letter that enhance its central theme: unity in diversity in Christ.

The message of Ephesians—that God has removed all social barriers that divide the human family, thereby creating one new humanity in Christ, in the church, in the home—must be proclaimed and practiced in the church, for it faces a malpractice suit from an unbeliving, skeptical world.

Putting into practice the message of Ephesians, however, is one of the most difficult tasks the Christian church faces, because Satan has summoned the very powers of hell to oppose the Christian individually and the church collectively from accomplishing this endeavor. How to oppose these nonhuman powers in order to accomplish God's purpose for the church is the purpose of the last section of this letter, and the theme of this chapter—"armed for the struggle."

Our strength is in the Lord

Paul begins this last section (Ephesians 6:10-24) with the

word *finally*. He has shared with the Gentile believers much about God's plan for His church. Through Jesus Christ, God has broken down all social and religious barriers that create hostility, segregation, and inequality in the human family. The result is a new humanity in Christ, guided by a different set of principles, motivated by a different spirit, and moved into action by a different end goal, God's kingdom. All of this distinguishes God's new humanity from the rest of the world. The difference is Christ. All who have made a conscious choice to accept Christ constitute the church, the embodiment of this new humanity, this new family in Christ. The church is to be a community of believers that reveals God's purpose for the human family in every attitude, action, and decision.

Hostility ends in the church, not the world. The world does not know Christ, and, therefore, it does not accept His "foreign policy" toward the nations. But the church does, for it is comprised of people from all nations who have considered what Christ offers and have decided to live by His commandments. Things that normally divide people in the world are no longer to divide them in the church.

Thus, within the family of God there is no dividing wall of hostility—or at least there shouldn't be. Wherever that wall exists in the church, it is condemning evidence that the church has ceased to be the church, no matter what it professes! " 'Lord, Lord, did we not prophesy in your name, and cast out demons in your name, and do many mighty works in your name?' . . . 'I never knew you' " (Matthew 7:22, 23), the Lord says. Why does God reject a people who claim to be His, who claim to be Christian, and who bear His name? The answer is given in the prior verse: "Not everyone who says to me, 'Lord, Lord,' shall enter the kingdom of heaven, but he who does *the will of my Father* who is in heaven" (Matthew 7:21, emphasis supplied).

There is more to being a Christian than just doing good works. The Laodiceans do good works, but God is ready to spit them out, for their works are nauseating. It is not the doing of works that determines whether one is a Christian, but the *kinds* of works one does—works reflective of the will of God.

And what is the difference between these two types of works? Jesus declared in the Sermon on the Mount, "Let your light so shine before [others], that they may see your good works and *give glory to your Father* who is in heaven" (Matthew 4:16, emphasis supplied). The difference lies in who gets the glory. We can find ourselves doing all kinds of good deeds, all for our own self-enhancement, whether that self be our individual selves or our collective institutional self. The result is much talk about ourselves, how great a church we are, and how much we have accomplished, statistic piled upon statistic, all reminiscent of Nebuchadnezzar: "Is not this great Babylon, which I have built by my mighty power?" (Daniel 4:30).

God looks at all that self-exaltation done under the cover of His name, and He is ready to vomit. " 'I never knew you; depart from me, you evildoers' " (Matthew 7:23).

Unity in the church does not mean uniformity, however, for each of us has different spiritual gifts that are to be employed in the upbuilding of the body of Christ. Concern for others guides our moral behavior as Christians, as we emulate the moral standard of the church, Jesus Christ.

This unity is also to be manifested in the home, in domestic relationships, where both husband and wife submit to one another as a result of their submission to Christ, the true Head of the home.

But this submission to one another, arising out of humility, "with patience, forbearing one another in love" (Ephesians 4:2), eager to maintain the unity of the Spirit in the bond of peace—with one body, one Spirit, one hope, one Lord, one faith, one baptism, one God and Father of us all—is most difficult to maintain in our own strength, for the opposition is great.

Thus, Paul declares, "Finally." He says, in effect, "Let me share with you one final point—how all of this is possible. Then he continues: "Be strong in the Lord and in the strength of His might" (chap. 6:10). The strength to accomplish the task comes from the Lord, not from ourselves. And how do we become strong in the Lord? By "[putting] on the whole armor of God, that [we] may be able to stand against the wiles of the devil" (verse 11). What does *wiles* mean? The Greek word *methaodeia* means "method." Satan has a method, a strategy, a plan all worked out to perpetuate division among God's people. Things do not happen by coincidence. The continual superiority of one group over other groups in society and in the church is not mere happenstance, one of those things that just "worked out that way." Apartheid in South Africa did not just happen. Racial bigotry and cultural insensitivity are not random experiences, but are socially constructed. And their manifestation in society and in the church is not mere coincidence. The subordination of women in the home, in the church, and in society did not come about by chance. No! All these social inequities are part of a well-laid strategy, a perfected plan, a diabolical method, conceptualized and instigated by Satan, but implemented by people to perpetuate power and control. To such Jesus declares, "I never knew you; depart from me, you evildoers" (Matthew 7:23).

Why the devil?

Why the devil? I thought it was Black South Africans fighting White South Africans, North Americans against Central Americans, East versus West, Communists against Capitalists, Jews against Gentiles, slaves against free, males against females.

No! That is the cosmetic struggle—what we see on the surface. The real struggle lies behind the scenes. "We are not contending against flesh and blood, but against the principalities, against the powers, against the world rulers of this present darkness, against the spiritual hosts of wickedness in the heavenly places" (chap. 6:12). Our struggle to maintain unity in diversity in Christ is not against mere human power, but against the forces of hell. Satan himself is leading this attack against the church. It is not just Black against White; it is not just clergy in conflict with laity; it is not just men preventing women from becoming all that God intends them to be. The struggle is greater; the battle lines are deeper into the stronghold of the enemy, for the enemy is Satan himself. No wonder the conflict is so great and victories in this area so few!

Recall Peter and the victory he gained as a result of his experience with Cornelius. Yet years later in Antioch, that victory slipped away from him the day he separated himself from the Gentiles when several Jews came up from Jerusalem (see Galatians 2:11-14).

Too often the church is like Peter. We make fine declarations of faith, excellent pronouncements, and outstanding speeches. Yet when the dust settles, we are still in our separate camps of segregation, racism, classism, and sexism. And no wonder, for Satan himself is leading the opposition!

What are we to do? I offer three suggestions.

First, we need a new understanding of sin. As stated earlier, sin is more than a personal infraction of God's holy law. It is also a social infraction of human relationships. As Christians we live in two dimensions: a vertical dimension focused on God, and a horizontal dimension focused on human need. Sin impacts both dimensions, in the sense that sin against God strikes at the personal level, while sin against humankind strikes at the social plane.

Jesus called the vertical dimension the "first commandment"—love to God (see Matthew 22:37, 38), or what James refers to as "faith" (see James 2). The second dimension, the horizontal, Jesus called the "second" commandment—love of neighbor (see Matthew 22:39), or what James calls "works" (see James 2). James keeps these two dimensions in balance when he declares:

> What does it profit, my brethren, if a man says he has faith but has not works? Can faith save him? If a brother or sister is ill-clad and in lack of daily food, and one of you says to them, "Go in peace, be warmed and filled," without giving them the things needed for the body, what does it profit? So faith by itself, if it has no works, is dead.
>
> For as the body apart from the spirit is dead, so faith apart from works is dead (James 2:14-17, 26).

To which Jesus adds: " 'On these two commandments depend all the law and the prophets' " (Matthew 22:40). Everything depends on a balanced approach to ministry—the divine and the human, the personal and the social.

Second, the church needs to view its role in society in a different light. James M. Gustafson declares, "Many make the explicit or tacit assumption that the Church is so absolutely unique in character that it can be understood only in its own private language."[1] Such a view overlooks the fact that the church is not only a divine institution, the body of Christ, but also a human institution with social, political, and economic dimensions. Yet in clarifying the nature of the church we define it only from a biblical perspective. Thus our understanding of the church is confined to a theological dimension only. All the while, the church as a social institution, functioning in society and within history, continues to affect people's lives politically, economically, and socially. But because we define the church only theologically, no mention is made of its political, economic, and social sins.

The nature of God's kingdom is to break down all dividing walls that separate people, be they racial, cultural, sexual, social, political, or economic. We must destroy anything that might keep God's children from becoming the new humanity in Christ. The church must see its role in society in a new light, one in which it does battle against this evil in the church and in society. Jesus told Peter, " 'On this rock I will build My church, and the gates of [hell] shall not prevail against it' " (Matthew 16:18, NKJV). Often this passage is read from a wrong perspective. We tend to view the church as a "fortress" being attacked by the "gates of hell," and the clarion cry from pupits throughout the world is that the "gates of hell" shall not prevail against the church.

We've got it all backward. Have you ever seen "gates" attacking anything? Gates are there to keep in or out. The church is not the one being attacked. Rather, the church is the one doing the attacking. Like the rock that destroyed Nebuchadnezzar's image (see Daniel 2:34, 35), the church takes the battle for justice to the very gates of hell—to the root and source of evil—and brings liberty to the captives and those in prison (see Luke 4:18). And the gates of hell "shall not prevail," (shall withstand) the attack. The church must see its mission from the divine perspective, not the human. Instead of a fortress cowering against the enemy, we need to view the church as a "flying fortress," much like the B-29 bombers of World War II, taking the battle against evil right to the stronghold of the enemy. This is the true picture of the church, militant against evil and not complacent in conformity.

The problem is that we are not only a cowering church but also an *escaping* church—escaping behind texts like, "My kingdom is not of this world" (John 18:36, NKJV). We have wrongly interpreted this text to mean that the church should not get involved in social issues, for it is not of this world. Rather, as Christians we should patiently endure the hardships, contradictions, and injustices of this world until that time God ushers in the next. This is an exegetical cop-out! The key word in this text is *of.* The Greek word is *ek,* meaning "out of," "from," "the point of origin." Jesus means that His kingdom does not *proceed* out of this world. The principles that govern His kingdon come from a heavenly world. If they came from this world, then Christ's servants would fight. However, His kingdom originates in another world. Christ's servants *behave differently,* because they are guided by principles of action from another world.

Jesus never preached or practiced an *escapist* theology. Rather, He stressed a theology that *revolutionized* life here in the old earth, in preparation for the new earth.

Third, the church is to take on the whole armor of God. Paul declares, "Take the whole armor of God, that you may be able to withstand the evil day, and having done all, to stand" (Ephesians 6:13). Since our struggle is not against flesh and blood, or mere human power, our weapons must also be different. If we were fighting against humans, then we could use human weapons: voice and vote, pen and pressure, attitude and action. But we struggle not so much against humans as against principalities, powers, and the prince of darkness. Against such forces a new weapon is needed, greater than any strategic defense initiative. For this truly is a "star war," a war between the bright and morning Star—Christ, and the

141

son of the morning, the lightbearer—Lucifer. In such a battle, the weapons must be divine and not human. That is why we need "the armor of God" (see Ephesians 6:14-17).

The armor of God

Interpreters throughout history have envisioned Paul in his prison cell, chained to a Roman legionnaire, using the armor of the legionnaire to describe how the Christian must also be dressed and armed for the struggle.

But I suggest that it is not a Roman legionnaire Paul has in mind when he describes the Christian's battle attire, but the Commander of the army of the Lord, Jesus Christ Himself, who in full battle gear revealed Himself to Joshua before he took Jericho (see Joshua 5:13-15). As a good Jew, Paul was acquainted with the Scriptures and their depiction of God in full military regalia. Notice how the Scriptures descibe God:

Paul's desciption	**The Old Testament description**
Loins girded with truth.	"Righteousness shall be the girdle of his waist, and faithfulnes the girdle of his loins" (Isaiah 11:5).
Put on the breastplate of righteousness.	"He put on righteousness as a breastplace" (Isaiah 59:17).
Feet shod with the gospel of peace	"How beautiful upon the mountains are the feet of him who brings good tidings, who publishes peace, who brings good tidings of good, who publishes salvation, who says to Zion, 'Your God reigns' " (Isaiah 52:7).
Take the shield of faith.	"My shield is with God, who saves the upright in heart" (Psalm 7:10).
Take the helmet of salvation.	"He put on . . . a helmet of salvation upon his head" (Isaiah 59:17).

The sword of the Spirit, which is the Word of God.	"He shall smite the earth with the rod of his mouth" (Isaiah 11:4). (Here is the sword, which is the Word.)

Thus, what Paul described here is not some Roman legionnaire, but Jesus Christ Himself, the Commander of the heavenly host. A Roman soldier, the symbol of one of the greatest oppressive powers in history, would have been incongrous with the gospel Paul was preaching. Paul describes, not some human soldier, but Christ, for Christ alone is the One who can defeat Satan. After all, it is God's armor that we are to put on, not some human armor. This is precisely what Paul tells us in Romans 13:12, "Let us then cast off the works of darkness and put on the armor of light." What is this "armor of light"? Paul gives us the answer in verse 14: "Put on the Lord Jesus Christ."

That is what it means to put on the armor of God—to put on Christ. Without Christ, all endeavors in this spiritual struggle will go down as efforts in futility.

Does this mean that the Christian does not get involved in human struggles for justice, but simply regards it all as a spiritual struggle to be waged alone by God? No! Absolutely not! The Christian is dressed for battle, not for bed. This is Paul's thought in Romans 13:11-14:

> You know what hour it is, how it is full time now for you to wake from sleep. For salvation is nearer to us now than when we first believed; the night is far gone, the day is at hand. Let us then cast off the works of darkness [cast off your bedclothes, cast off your pajamas, cast off your clothes of leisure] and put on the armor of light; let us conduct ourselves becomingly as in the day, not in reveling and drunkenness, not in dabauchery and licentiousness, not in quarreling and jealousy. [In other words, throw off your party clothes.] But put on the Lord Jesus Christ, and make no provision for the flesh, to gratify its desires.

Our armor is *righteousness*. But here we have a problem, because we have divorced righteousness from justice. The English and German languages are dualistic in the distinctions they make between *justice and righteousness,* whereas the Hebrew makes no such dichotomies. Righteousness and justice are the one and only *justitiá.* In Spanish there is no word for righteousness. It is all one word, *justicia.* This division in English and German has caused the church to focus its understanding of righteousness on a theoretical knowledge of God, based on a personal spiritual righteousness that is concerned with self at the expense of social justice that is concerned with others. We talk of righteousness but not of justice. Yet this armor of righteousness is an armor of *justice.*

Thus, the Christian must be involved in liberation issues. We must develop a "worldly theology—a theology that not only opens our eyes to the social misery of the world but also teaches us to understand it better and to transform it,"[2] for *"God so loved the world* that He gave . . ." (John 3:16, emphasis supplied). Thus, the struggle of other human beings is also our struggle, for injustice anywhere is injustice everywhere.

But we don't go off half-cocked. Paul declares, "Pray at all times in the Spirit, with all prayer and supplication. To that end keep alert with all perseverence, making supplication for all the saints" (Ephesians 6:18). Prayer to the Christian is like radio contact to the soldier. Without constant communication from the command post, a soldier will not know his position or what to do, and may stray into the enemy fire or, even worse, may end up shooting at his own forces.

One of the worst results of the Vietnam War was an action called "friendly fire." Friendly fire was a situation in which our soldiers were killed by *their own* bullets, as a result of miscalculations, bad judgment, wrong coordinates, lack of or wrong communications, or just plain stupidity. But whether our soldiers were killed by Vietnamese bullets or American bullets, they were dead just the same. Bullets do not discriminate. Thus, radio communication is important.

The same thing happens in the church. A lot of people are being killed by "friendly fire"—verbal bullets that we call "constructive criticism" but that destroy just the same. You can't shoot your fellow Christians, however, if you are praying for them. Have you ever tried to criticize someone for whom you were praying? Kind of hard, isn't it? You can't shoot the pastor if you are praying for him. That is why Paul says, "[Pray] also for me, that utterance may be given me in opening my mouth boldy to proclaim the mystery of the gospel, . . . that I may declare it boldly, as I ought to speak" (verse 19).

This is how we are to be armed for the struggle—by putting on Christ. Only when we put on Christ can we live out the unity that Christ desires to see in His church. The church's purpose for existence is to put on Christ so that we can manifest in our daily relations this unity in diversity in Christ. The result will be the final words with which Paul closes Ephesians: "Peace be to the brethren, and love with faith, from God the Father and the Lord Jesus Christ" (verse 23). "Peace to the brethren"! That is the outcome of Christian unity.

And how is this peace maintined? Paul says that it is by grace. "Grace be with all who love our Lord Jesus Christ with love undying" (verse 24).

Notice that we are to love Jesus with an undying love. That is how Jesus loved us, and now we are to love Him in return. He loved us with *dying* love; we are to love Him with love *undying*.

---

1. James M. Gustafson, *Treasure in Earthen Vessels: The Church As a Human Community* (Chicago: The University of Chicago Press, 1961), p. 100.

2. Cornel West, Foreword to the book by Franz J. Hinklelammert, *The Ideological Weapons of Death: A Theological Critique of Capitalism* (Maryknoll, N.Y.: Orbis Books, 1987) .

Sixteen

Is This Unity in Diversity Possible?

The central message of Paul's letter to the Ephesians is that the "mystery of Christ," the incorporation of Jew and Gentile into one new humanity in Christ, is to be made visible in the church. In other words, unity in diversity in Christ is possible in the church.

If this is the case, then why is such unity not visible, for the most part, in the church today? Let me suggest a couple of reasons. One is that as Christians we tend to hold a view of God as *exclusive*. The Bible portrays God as holy, high and lifted up, before whom humans shrink away in fear (see Isaiah 6:1-5). Rudolf Otto called this experience the "mysterium tremenum."[1] One of the problems with present-day Christianity is that we have not experienced this sense of God, One who because of holiness rejects evil in all its forms and is removed from it, but because of love draws close to human beings, the object of God's divine love.

Because of its failure to experience the "holy" from the perspective of the divine, the church has developed a distorted understanding of holiness as an irrational, pietistic behavior that shuns those who might be different. The result is rejection of others and glorification of self-righteousness. Such a distortion results in a view of God as exclusive. We need to develop an *inclusive* view of God as One who shuns evil but loves the evildoer. The world is longing for such an inclusive God. Failing to see this God among Christians who are exclusive in their attitudes and actions toward others yet greedy in their graft for gain, many today reject God outright.

A second reason why this oneness in not made manifest in the church is what I call a "theology of neglect." We have neglected to teach as doctrine *the organizing principle of Christianity:* "There is neither Jew nor Greek [no division based on race and ethnicity], there is neither slave nor free [no division based on status and social class], there is neither male nor female [no division based on sex and gender]; for you are all *one* in Christ Jesus" (Galatians 3:28, emphasis supplied).

From grade school on, like many other Christians, Adventists teach their children through campaigns, oratorical contests, and media material that the use of alcohol, tobacco, and drugs is morally and physically wrong and that such usage constitutes a *sin.* We have never done the same with racism, classism, and sexism. Can you imagine the impact on our children that poster campaigns, oratorical and essay contests, and films on unity in diversity in Christ would have? We are great at developing "five-day plans" to stop smoking and producing such classic films as *One in Twenty Thousand,* which graphically depicts the surgical removal of cancer. How about five-day plans and films on the removal of the cancer of racism, classism, and sexism from our lives? We need to instill in our youth those divine values that will counteract racism, classism, and sexism.

The reason for failure here is that we ourselves are guilty. Let me illustrate. If Seventh-day Adventists ate pork, smoked tobacco, and drank alcoholic beverages, as some Christians do, we would not be able to preach our strong health message. But because racism, classism, and sexism are practiced, there is very little preaching against these evils. Our Christian practice in this area reflects the practice of our society, which lives by the principles of Satan's kingdom. Thus, we may be drinking at "broken cisterns," while the living water of the gospel is seeping through the cracks of racism, classism, and sexism in the church.

We need to return to the primitive godliness of the early church:

> The company of those who believed were of one heart and soul, and no one said that any of the things which he possessed was his own, but they had everything in common. And with great power the apostles gave their testimony to the resurrection of the Lord Jesus, and great grace was upon them all. There was not a needy person among them, for as many as were possessors of lands or houses sold them, and brought the proceeds of what was sold and laid it at the apostles' feet; and distribution was made to each as any had need. (Acts 4:32-35).

This passage tells us that Christians in the early church had two basic characteristics:

1. They experienced love for one another in the context of a warm, caring, compassionate community.

2. They took care of the needy within their community.

The problem with our churches is that we often lack in these two characteristics, and many have left the church as a result.

In November 1978 our society was shocked by the news of the Jim Jones massacre in Guyana. Many of those who chose to follow Jones were Christians. Why did they leave their faith to join a cult? What attracted them to the Peoples Temple? Mel White, a film producer, decided to investigate the question. He interviewed defectors and found that the churches out of which the defectors came prior to joining the Peoples Temple lacked the two characteristics of the early church: compassion within a caring community for those inside and outside.

White goes on to record the testimony of several defectors. I want to focus on just two. The first is Jeannie Mills. White introduces Jeannie's testimony with the following statement:

> For fifteen years Jeannie worked hard in her church as a teacher and in other volunteer capacities. She had struggled in the early years of her marriage to put her husband through

Bible school, so that he might become a minister in their denomination. When she was twenty-nine her marriage failed. Jeannie and her first husband were divorced. Eventually she expressed her desire to remarry, and so began her journey to the Peoples Temple.

Jeannie's testimony:

The church fathers called me and suggested that they understood how these things go, but by the rules of the church, the first person to remarry was committing adultery, and that I could save everybody a great deal of embarrassment if I would just quietly withdraw my membership from the church. This left me without a church. I was very concerned about my children's souls. I still sent them to Christian schools, and I asked my mother if she still was praying, and to please pray for the souls of my children, but I felt so alone. Then I got to thinking. When I was in church where we were all going to heaven, we hardly talked to each other on earth. How was it that when we sit in heaven in a twinkling of an eye everything will change? Will everybody start loving and caring up there? Or in heaven am I going to still feel like an outcast—like I am never really good enough? After they asked me to leave the church I went to churches, all kind of different churches. And in every church, maybe the minister would say hello to me, if I stood in line. In some churches maybe a deaconess or a greeter would come up and welcome me. Sometimes someone would share a hymnal with me. When I left the service that was it. It was as if I worked really hard, if I went back again, and again, and again, maybe I would find a church family there. But I didn't have the energy to try. I was so turned off in every church, I left because nobody cared. Nobody cared that I, a human being with feelings, thoughts and emotions, came into their doors. And that is when I went to Peoples Temple.

Everybody seemed so caring and loving. They hugged us and made us welcomed. So many said they liked us, and wanted us to come back. And after the first service many people sent letters. The church even sent a box of candy.

Who was this Jeannie Mills? She was a Seventh-day Adventist! Jeannie says:

I attended and taught in my church's Christian education program from childhood. When I was eighteen years old I was leader of the Pathfinder Club, which had over fifty kids in it, and I had twenty two adults working under me. I could give you an answer from the Bible for any question. I knew the Bible backwards and forwards. At one point in my life, the minister tried to send me to college to become a Bible Worker. I was very dedicated to the church.[2]

I got in contact with Jeannie Mills in early February of 1980 and asked her to come and speak at All Nations Church. She agreed to come on May 10, 1980, with her husband Al Mills, the photographer of the Peoples Temple. On February 15, Jeannie sent me a book, her autobiography, *Six Years With God: Life Inside Rev. Jim Jones's Peoples Temple* (Jim Jones regarded himself as "God"). On the flyleaf she wrote, "To Pastor Rosado: Always question authority! Jeannie Mills." On February 26, Jeannie, her husband Al, and their daughter Daphene were slain in their apartment by a death squad that Jim Jones had left behind to do away with defectors. She never made it to All Nations Church.

Grace Stoen:

Her mother was Mexican, her family was Maltese. She was a beautiful olive-complected woman, yet the discrimination she experienced in a white parochial school in San Francisco, because she was poor and not quite white, made her feel unloved and uncared for in her church, and a perfect candidate for membership in Peoples Temple.

Grace Stoen's testimony is one of the clearest statements why the Christian church must exemplify unity in diversity in Christ in a multicultural setting:

I remember walking into my Catholic school and the Irish kids would call me a nigger. When I told my parents they told me not to listen to them. My mother was a Mexican, and all her life she had been told that Mexicans were dirty and that they were no good, so she worked doubly hard to make sure we had neat, clean uniforms. One day when I was in the second grade, I played kickball on the way to parochial school, and my shoes got scuffed. A nun made me stand in front of the class, and proceeded to humiliate me. She said I was filthy and why would I come to school looking like that. We lived on the fringe of a very rich parish. The rich and the white were always favored. Once in the second grade they expected us kids to bring envelopes with money in them. We didn't have any money. But they still asked me why I didn't put any money in the envelope? I was in the second grade and being put up for not having money in my envelope. Money was all they talked about. They wanted people to give fifty dollars. They had plaques on the wall saying who had given five hundred dollars, and who had given one thousand dollars. When I was eighteen I still didn't have five hundred dollars, but I finally realized why it was that there was all those special memorials for people who gave money, but nobody befriended me. I spent ten years of my life in that church, one day a week, and I never knew anybody. All that I saw was these cliques and the strong, white Irish thing, so I quit. When I went to Peoples Temple they weren't taking any offerings. I'll never forget seeing all the races, black and white together. You always heard it couldn't be done, and they couldn't get along. Yet, at the Temple there were educated and illiterate, there were middle class and poor, there was everything there, and I was really touched by the warmness of the people. You didn't see people whispering, you know, talking about each other. Everybody was open, warm, open-hearted and getting to know one another, and I felt that my heart was just taken in by those beautiful people.[3]

I am often asked, "Is it really possible to bring about such racial unity?" My answer is an unqualified *yes*! And the reason for this is Paul's letter to the Ephesians, the whole theme of which is the incorporation of Jew and Gentile into one new humanity in Christ, which he calls the "mystery of Christ." This "mystery," this bringing together of different ethnic groups into one body, is to be made manifest *through the church,* where God will make the final manifestation of the gospel—His character of love—which unites Christ's family into a visible oneness, to the chagrin and exposure of the principalities and powers of evil.

The major problem of the church

The major problem confronting the early church, which threatened the validity of the gospel in the first century, was the conflict between Jew and Gentile. The book of Acts and the majority of Paul's letters deal with this problem. It threatened to divide the church in the first century (see Acts 6:1). It caused Peter problems with church leaders over the conversion of Cornelius (see Acts 11:1-18). The first Christian church council was convened specifically to deal with this matter (see Acts 15). Paul's rebuke to Peter in Antioch was over the same issue (see Galatians 2:11-14), and the entire letter to the Ephesians focuses on this difficulty. The problem was that many Jewish Christians still clung to the socially divisive teachings and practices of Pharisaic Judaism, with its built-in ethnocentrism, segregationism, racial and sexual prejudice, discrimination, and religious bigotry. The problem was primarily with the Jews, and it so dominated the early church that an entire religio-political party developed within first-century Christianity: the Judaizers, whose sole mission was to get Gentiles to live like Jews.

The problem was finally resolved by an appeal to the gospel, in which Paul made it clear that:

> [Christ] is our peace, who made us both one, and has broken down the dividing wall of hostility, by abolishing in his flesh the law of commandments and ordinances, that he might create in himself one new [person] in place of the two, so making peace, and might reconcile us both to God in one body through the cross, thereby bringing the hostility to an end (Ephesians 2:14-16).

That was the problem of the early church and its solution. The major problem confronting the last-day church, which is also threatening the validity of the gospel, is a resurgence of the old problem, but in a new garb and on a global scale—the conflict between Whites and non-Whites. It has divided society into the Black and White, East and West, North and South, First World and Third World. The problem is essentially the same, in that most people converted to Christianity have still hung on to the socially divisive values and practices of the White Western world, with its built-in ethnocentrism, segregationism, racial and sexual prejudice, discrimination, and religious and ideological bigotry. And like the Judaizers of old, many White Westerners are imposing a cultural and religious baggage on the rest of the world that has nothing to do with the gospel in an effort to get them to live like Westerners. The result has been, at worst, a rejection of the gospel, and at best, a divided church.

The problem, as of old, can be resolved only by an appeal to the gospel, and a manifestation of that appeal in the practice of the church. The fleshing out of this manifestation in the church needs to be one of the primary focuses of the church. As long as this oneness is not made visible in the church, the church has no message. Wasn't this what Jesus said: "I in them, and Thou in Me, that they may be perfected in unity, that the world may know that Thou didst send Me, and didst love them, even as Thou didst love Me" (John 17:23, NASB)?

In 1 Corinthians 12:12-27 Paul speaks of the church as one body with many members. In verses 24 and 25 he gives us the "divine intention" on how to structure the church for effective ministry: "God has so composed the body, giving the greater honor to the inferior part, that there may be no discord in the body, but that the members may have the same care for one another." Talk about conflict resolution within the caring church—here is the key! God's intention for His church is that it be structured in such a manner that those regarded as inferior be given the greater honor, that there may be no discord within the body. God is not talking about some future time in glory, but now, in our present social reality.

The early church reflected this caring oneness, as we have read in Acts, and so will the last church. Ellen White says, "Before the final visitation of God's judgments upon the earth

153

there will be among the people of the Lord such a revival of *primitive godliness* as has not been witnessed since apostolic times.[4] The godliness of the early church consisted, among other factors, in the *koinonia*—the fellowship—that sense of caring community manifested in a oneness, that all the believers from different ethnic groups had in common with each other. That, more than anything else, according to Jesus' prayer in John 17, will convince the world that Jesus is Lord!

The manifestation of such "primitive godliness" needs to be the central aspect of the mission of the church. The question is: Will the church be faithful to its mission?

Conclusion

One of the things that I enjoy most in viewing the Olympics is the contrast between the opening and closing ceremonies. In the opening ceremonies the athletes come parading into the stadium by countries, under their separate flags. In the closing ceremonies, the athletes once again enter the stadium, but this time as *one group,* with no national divisions. Why? *Because the competition is over!*

This is the message of Ephesians, a message that the world does not understand and the church has failed to manifest: that because of Christ, the competition is over. Christ has competed on our behalf, the gold has been won, and we are all victors, for God has no losers.

The message that the church needs to give to a dying world in its proclamation and practice is that in Christ, *the competition is over!*

---

1. Rudolf Otto, *The Idea of the Holy* (New York: Oxford University Press, 1958).
2. Mel White, *Deceived* (Old Tappan, N.J.: Fleming H. Revell Company, 1979), pp. 15-19.
3. *Ibid.,* pp. 19-21.
4. Ellen G. White, *The Great Controversy* (Mountain View, Calif.: Pacific Press, 1911), p. 464, emphasis supplied.

Addendum

The Healing of the Nations

The material in this addendum is most important for the subject matter of this book, but since it does not specifically arise out of a study of Ephesians, I have placed it at the end, as an added excursus to exercise the reader's mental faculties. A word of caution to the reader. The thoughts expressed here are my conjectures, based on certain statements from Ellen G. White and scientific research. They should in no way be taken as gospel truth, but as human speculation.

As stated in the second chapter, on the definition of racism, color is merely the excuse to justify much of the oppression in the world today. In view of the importance of color in differentiating human beings, when did the human race cross "the color line"? Or stated differently, since the entire human family proceeded from a single set of parents, Adam and Eve, it would seem natural to expect that the first generations of human beings were essentially of the same color. When did color start making a difference in the human family?

More than likely, after the confusion of languages at the Tower of Babel, when God dispersed the various newly created language groups throughout the entire globe (see Genesis 11:1-9). Scientists have long recognized that geography and climate affect color. "Skin color, for instance, is a minor adaptation to climate—black in Africa for protection from the sun, white in Europe to absorb ultraviolet radiation that helps produce vitamin D." It doesn't take long in the history of the human race "for skin color to change."[1] With the changing of the seasons and the world climates after the Flood, God simply varied the amount of melanin—the brownish-black pigmentation that all except albinos have—depending on where people settled, as a protection against the sun. God thus performed a protective miracle.

The original color of humankind

This raises two interesting questions: What was the original color of Adam and Eve? And what color are we going to be in heaven? The word *Adam,* meaning "man," in the Akkadian signifies "dark, red soil."[2] The fact that Adam was formed from the "dust of the ground" (Genesis 2:7, KJV) would also suggest that the original color of the first human beings was the color of the earth—dark, reddish brown. The latest scientific evidence with regard to the origin of the human race concurs with this. It comes from molecular biology's research of mitochondrial DNA, which is located in the baby's placenta and can be inherited only from the mother.[3] Scientists are now finding that the genes retain a more complete record of human history than do fossil records.[4] The findings suggest that the human race descended from a single woman and that she was an African. Other findings show that " 'there are really very few genetic differences among cultures.' Stoneking says, 'In terms of our mitochondrial DNA, we're much more closely related than almost any other vertebrate or mammalian species. You find New Guineans whose DNA is closer to other Asians' than to other New Guineans'.' "[5]

The implications of this for the concept of "one human family" are tremendous. Stephen Jay Gould, a Harvard paleontologist, says: "It makes us realize that all human beings, despite differences in external appearance, are really members of a single entity that's had a very recent origin in one place. There is a kind of biological brotherhood that's much more profound than we ever realized."[6] Such a realization reinforces the central theme and truth of Ephesians—that if the human family is *one by creation,* then all the more reason why the church, the embodiment of the redeemed, must be one by redemption.

These findings suggest that Adam and Eve were dark skinned, more like native American Indians in color, and definitely not white as usually portrayed. Ellen G. White reaches a similar conclusion when she declares:

> As Adam came forth from the hand of his Creator, he was of noble hight (sic), and of beautiful symmetry. He was more than twice as tall as men now living upon the earth, and was well proportioned. His features were perfect and beautiful. *His complexion was neither white, nor sallow, but ruddy, glowing with the rich tint of health.* Eve was not quite as tall as Adam. Her head reached a little above his shoulders. She, too, was noble— perfect in symmetry, and very beautiful.[7]

If our first parents, as they came forth from the Creator's hands, were dark skinned, what color will we be in heaven, in view of the various shades and hues we see in the world today? A statement from *The Desire of Ages* may move us toward an answer to this question.

> As Jesus rose from the dead, so those who sleep in Him are to rise again. We shall know our friends, even as the disciples knew Jesus. They may have been deformed, diseased, or disfigured, in this mortal life, and they rise in perfect health and symmetry; yet in the glorified body their identity will be perfectly preserved. Then shall we know even as also we are known. 1 Cor. 13:12. In the face radiant with the light shining from the face of Jesus, *we shall recognize the lineaments of those we love.*[8]

This statement makes it very clear that at the Resurrection we will be able to recognize each other. Now if I as a brown Hispanic all of a sudden appeared as a White or Black in the resurrection, those who knew me on this earth might not recognize me. The same would be true of a black- or a white-skinned person, suggesting that at the Resurrection, the change from mortality to immortality, which will take place "in a moment, in the twinkling of an eye" (1 Corinthians 15:52), will not affect our skin color and biological differences, but only our mortality.

Does this mean that for the rest of eternity the genetic differences that came upon the human race as a result of sin will remain? No, I don't believe so. I believe that a gradual process of transformation will take place that will return the redeemed of the human race to the physical and genetic characteristics Adam and Eve possessed at creation. Let me explain.

The healing of the nations

In Revelation 22 we find a description of what life in the new earth will be like, and of the central location of the tree of life in the New Jerusalem with its twelve kinds of fruit, yielding its fruit each month" (verse 2). In the next verse we find a most interesting statement: "the leaves of the tree were for the *healing of the nations*" (emphasis supplied). What is this? And what does it mean?

Apparently there is a "disease" among the nations that only the leaves of the tree of life can heal. What is this "disease"? It is not sin, as there will be no sin in the new earth. It is not physical deformities, as these would have been corrected at the resurrection. It has to be something that brought "sickness" to the nations, and from which the nations need "healing." And what is that? It is the biological and racial features that differentiate the human family.

When one studies human history closely, one sees that the things that have brought on more evil, wars, genocide, and inhumanity of humankind toward humankind are the racial and biological differences among human beings. These slight differences have led many groups throughout history to believe that they are superior to other groups, and they have sought to destroy these others or in some way to limit their human existence. Recall the results of the European expansion in the sixteenth century, which not only reshaped the world, but eventually turned the world into First World, Second World, and Third World. Recall the rape and plunder of native populations in the lands of conquest—the Indians in the Americas and the Blacks in Africa. Recall the involuntary removal of millions of people from Africa to become the machines of a preindustrial society in the new world. Recall the wholesale destruction of millions of Jews in the gas chambers and ovens of Germany during World War II. Recall also the incarceration and placement in concentration camps in the United States of some 125,000 Japanese Americans, simply because they looked different and could possibly pose a threat to national security. The same was not done for Germans, against whom the war was also being fought!

These racial and biological differences will not be removed at the resurrection. However, as we partake of the fruit of the tree of life—"the antidote of death"[9]—and especially of the leaves of the tree, the process will begin of "healing the nations," or returning of the human race back to the physical stature and genetic characteristics of Adam and Eve as they were originally created. How long will the process take? I don't know. But eventually, as we eat the leaves of the tree, the physical characteristics that distinguish people from every nation will disappear. And we will continue to know each other, for the process of change will not be rapid. Eventually the human family will once again be *one*, in all that that entails.

---

1. Robert Cohen, *The Color of Man* (New York: Bantam Books, 1968); John Tierney, Lynda Wright, and Karen Springen, "The Search for Adam and Eve," *Newsweek* (January 11, 1988), p. 50.

2. Fritz Maass, "Adam," in G. Johannes Botterweck and Helmer Ringgren, *Theological Dictionary of the Old Testament* (Grand Rapids, Mich.: Wm. B. Eerdmans, 1974).

3. The definitive study here is the one by Rebecca L. Cann, Mark Stoneking, and Allan C. Wilson, "Mitochondrial DNA and Human Evolution," *Nature* 325 (January 1, 1987), pp. 31-36; cf. Jim Wainscoat, "Out of the garden of Eden," *Nature* 325 (January 1, 1987), p. 13; Jim Wainscoat, et. al, "Evolutionary relationships of human populations from an analysis of nuclear DNA polymorphisms," *Nature* 319, (February 6, 1986), pp. 491-493; cf. Tierney, Wright, and Springen, p. 50.

4. J. S. Jones and S. Rouhani, "How small was the bottleneck?" *Nature* 319 (February 6, 1986), p. 449.

5. Tierney, Wright, and Springen, p. 49.

6. *Ibid.*, p. 47.

7. Ellen G. White, *Spiritual Gifts* (Washington, D.C.: Review and Herald, 1945), vol. 3, p. 34, emphasis supplied.

8. Ellen G. White, *The Desire of Ages* (Mountain View, Calif.: Pacific Press, 1898), p. 804, emphasis supplied.

9. Ellen G. White, *Signs of the Times* (March 31, 1909); cited in *SDA Bible Commentary* (Washington, D.C.: Review and Herald, 1957), vol. 7, p. 988.